A MESSY, BROKEN, 40-DAY ADVENTURE
THROUGH THE BOOK OF JONAH

NOBODY LEFT OUT

WAVES OF GRACE

Copyright © 2022 Michael Murray

If you are interested in purchasing bulk copies of this book for group studies, discounts are available. Please contact Michael at nobodyleftout.net/contact for more information.

All rights reserved. No part of this publication may be reproduced, stored in a retrieval system, or transmitted in any form, or by any means—for example, electronic, photocopy, and recording—without the prior written permission of the publisher. The only exception is brief quotations in printed reviews. You may also use brief quotes in articles, books, and other teaching materials if this book is properly cited at the end.

Edited by Emily Lupfer

Scriptures are italicized and are taken from the following versions of the Bible:

THE HOLY BIBLE, NEW INTERNATIONAL VERSION®, NIV® Copyright © 1973, 1978, 1984, 2011 by Biblica, Inc.® Used by permission. All rights reserved worldwide.

The Holy Bible, New Living Translation (NLT), copyright © 1996, 2004, 2015 by Tyndale House Foundation. Used by permission of Tyndale House Publishers, Inc., Carol Stream, Illinois 60188. All rights reserved.

THE MESSAGE (MSG), copyright © 1993, 2002, 2018 by Eugene H. Peterson. Used by permission of NavPress. All rights reserved. Represented by Tyndale House Publishers, Inc.

Publishing services provided by

Paperback ISBN: 978-1-7379973-2-0
Hardback ISBN: 978-1-7379973-3-7

To all the lost Ninevehs and all the self-righteous Jonahs.

May we be reminded that we are all messy, broken people who need waves of grace.

Contents

Introduction: Setting Sail With Jonah 1
Pre-Boarding Tips (How To Use This Book) 3
Day 1: More Than a Fish Tale 6
Day 2: But Did It Really Happen? 9
Day 3: It's All About You 12
Day 4: Jonah on The Tonight Show 15
Day 5: Sending Nineveh a Peace Offering 17
Day 6: Setting off for a Distant Country 20
Day 7: "Please Send Someone Else!" 23
Day 8: Compassion in the Storm 26
Day 9: Waves of Grace 29
Day 10: "How Can You Sleep at a Time Like This?" 32
Day 11: Kindness & Patience in the Storm 35
Day 12: Religious Man Overboard! 38
Day 13: Sometimes Grace Smells Like Fish Guts 41
Day 14: Making the Most of Your Time in a Fish 44
Day 15: Messy Prayer 47
Day 16: Anatomy of a Fish Prayer 50
Day 17: But God 53
Day 18: Never Too Late to Return Home (Part I) 56
Day 19: Self-Righteous Prayer (Or, Did Jonah Just Diss the Ninevites?) 59
Day 20: Don't Go Diving for Buried Sins 62
Day 21: The God of Fresh Starts (The Adventure Continues...) 66
Day 22: Checking It off the To-Do List 69
Day 23: Is This Some Kind of Joke?! 72

Day 24: God Meets Us Where We're At 75
Day 25: The Devotional About Animals 78
Day 26: The God-Sized City in the Good Potter's Hands 82
Day 27: Jonah Got What He Wanted! 85
Day 28: But Did It Really Matter? 88
Day 29: The Reason Why There's a Fourth Chapter of Jonah 92
Day 30: Naming Our Enemies 95
Day 31: God Can't Win! 98
Day 32: When God Bends His Knee 101
Day 33: A Shelter of Self-Righteousness 104
Day 34: Sometimes Grace Feels Like a Sunburn 107
Day 35: Never Too Late to Return Home (Part II) 110
Day 36: The Wrong Way To Do Religion 113
Day 37: When God Loves My Enemy, It's Good News for Me 116
Day 38: Step Into Jonah's Shoes 119
Day 39: Maybe a Happy Ending After All? 123
Day 40: The Good Epilogue 126
The Next (Messy) Adventure Awaits 131
The Nobody Left Out Series 133
A Small Favor 135
About The Author 137
Special Thanks 139

Introduction:
Setting Sail With Jonah

Jonah is one of the most famous stories in the Bible. Even if you've never read it yourself, you've probably heard some version of it. It's a story we all *think* we know. Your classic "guy meets fish" story.

Guy meets fish. Fish swallows guy. Fish spits guy out on God's command.

For a long time, that's what I thought Jonah was about. It's a nice little Bible story with a clear moral: Obey God or get eaten by a whale.

But I was wrong!

About fifteen years ago, my church did a sermon series on the book of Jonah. As I took a closer look at the story, its beautiful message of grace began to… *surface*. (Yes, pun intended!) Jonah's story helped me see God's love in a new way, and it was a love that challenged me to love others.

As the years passed, I continued to return to Jonah's adventure. It wouldn't let me go. Each time I read it, I discovered a new layer of meaning. I became overwhelmed by the waves of grace found in the book. At its heart, Jonah's story is about how God doesn't want anyone left out. I don't know about you, but that's a message I desperately need to cling to each day.

Over the next 40 days, we're going to join Jonah on his adventure. We'll follow him as he runs from God and gets caught in a storm. We'll sink to the bottom of the ocean with him and wait for God's rescue. We'll walk with him begrudgingly into Nineveh—a city Jonah despises—and consider what (or who) it represents for us. And through it all, we'll get an up-close look at how God's love is big enough for everyone.

Jonah is a mess, and, if I'm being honest, that's the kind of Bible character I can relate to. He's stubborn, prideful, and thinks he knows it all. And yet, as I read the book of Jonah, I can't help but feel God smiling through the story. Not a sarcastic or sadistic smile, but a patient, loving smile. Because each time Jonah (or Michael) pitches a fit, or stomps his feet, or screams, or shuts down, God is there, ready to extend waves of grace.

Before I began writing this book, I asked people on my Facebook page what they thought the book of Jonah was about. My favorite response was from a woman named Jacqueline. She commented:

God loves us and has a very large sense of humor.

This made me laugh out loud because it's so true. I couldn't have put it better myself, Jacqueline!

As we set sail with Jonah, I hope you will see how much God loves you. As God meets Jonah in his mess, I pray you will know he is with you in yours.

Let this adventure be a fun reminder that God doesn't want anyone left out.

And that includes you!

Michael Murray

Pre-Boarding Tips
(How To Use This Book)

Note: If you've read any of my other books in the *Nobody Left Out* series, this chapter will probably sound familiar. Feel free to skim it if you need a refresher or skip it and get to the good stuff!

Before we officially set sail on our adventure with Jonah, I want to give you some tips on how to make the most of this devotional.

(By the way, the word *devotional* is simply a fancy, "churchy" word for a brief piece of writing, usually reflecting on a passage found in Scripture.)

Over the next 40 days, we'll walk through the story of Jonah chronologically, looking at it from all sides and perspectives. The book of Jonah is short, but it gives us a lot to think about. So we'll move through it slowly, looking at one small section at a time. Each day has a Bible reading to go along with the devotional. On most days, the reading will only be a few verses (except for Day 1, where we'll read the entire book to get a big-picture view of the story).

There's no "right way" to use this book. While I wrote it to be read over 40 days, go at whatever pace works best for you. Don't stress or get discouraged if you miss a day of reading! Just pick back up the next day. We don't earn "God points" by reading the Bible every day. There's nothing we can do to make God love us any more than he already does. Our goal is just to get to know him better!

Here are a few more reading tips:

→ As I mentioned, each day will have a designated Bible reading (usually from the book of Jonah). On some days, there will be a "supporting" passage of Scripture to read. These verses will provide more context for whatever we are discussing that day. I suggest taking some time to read both passages before reading the day's devotional.

→ If you're looking for a quick, easy way to access the Bible, consider downloading the YouVersion Bible App. Another great resource is BibleGateway.com.

→ There are many different Bible translations. I don't believe any single translation is the "best"—they all convey God's truth. (One of my favorite things to do is look at the same verse in multiple translations. It helps me understand it from a different perspective and gain new insight!) Throughout this book, I primarily quote from the New International Version (NIV) and New Living Translation (NLT). When reading the daily verses, feel free to use your preferred version. (You can even decide to go old school and whip out the King James Version. Thou art awesome!)

→ At the end of each devotional, I've included some questions to ponder. As with everything in this book, use them in whatever way is most helpful to you. My hope is that they will give you something to reflect on throughout the day. I want to encourage you to spend time with God as you think through them and come to your own conclusions about the story.

→ Each devotional should take about 10-15 minutes to complete (including reading the Bible verses). Here's my biggest piece of advice: Don't view reading the Bible as a chore. If you get through this devotional in 40 days, that's great. But you know what? If it takes you 40 years, that's okay too! If it helps to schedule the reading

PRE-BOARDING TIPS (HOW TO USE THIS BOOK)

at the same time every day, then do it. But if you're not a morning person, don't feel obligated to read it at 5 a.m. (At least get some coffee in you first!) Maybe lunch is a better time for you to read. Or right before bed. Do whatever works best for you.

Okay, that's it for the boring stuff. I think I see our friend Jonah buying a ticket and hopping aboard a ship. Let's catch up to him!

Day 1:
More Than a Fish Tale

Today's Bible Reading: Jonah 1-4

At the risk of offending you right on Day 1 of this devotional, I have a terrible confession to make: I have never seen the movie *E.T.* in its entirety. I've caught clips of it on television but I've never sat down to watch the film from start to finish. Despite this, one image flashes through my mind whenever I hear the word "E.T.": the iconic scene where Elliott and E.T. fly on a bicycle across the night sky, full moon shining in the background.

Now, imagine if I overheard two film buffs discussing *E.T.* and I said, "Oh, that's the movie all about bicycles!" They would look at me confused and say, "Well, sure, there's a bicycle scene in the movie... but that's not what the movie is *about*."

When you hear the word "Jonah," what flashes through your mind? For most of my life, it was the image of a whale. You've heard the outlandish tale before. *Jonah runs from God, a fish swallows him, and then he gets vomited out onto dry land.* Most retellings end there, even though there are still two more chapters left in the book!

In children's Bibles, the big fish is often portrayed as the main character of the story. But even as adults, our fascination with the fish can quickly become the main point of debate. Some people go to great lengths to prove that surviving three days in a fish is possible. Other people scoff at the implausibility of this tale, using it as evidence to dismiss the Bible as a joke. But both sides are missing the point of this beautiful story. The word "fish" appears only four times in the book of Jonah, and it's presented as one detail in a much larger narrative.

If we can stick a pin (or hook?) in the fish for a moment, we'll see that Jonah is an amazing story, but not because a man survived three days in a sea monster. This little book is amazing because it flips everything we'd expect from a Bible story upside down. Sometimes I can't believe it's in the Bible!

In the book of Jonah, a man of God looks like a fool, and pagans come out smelling like roses. In the book of Jonah, ships have personalities, prophets throw tantrums, and worms teach lessons. And, most importantly, in the book of Jonah, God tenderly reveals to us that his love is big enough for everyone. People who have never opened a Bible have one thing in common with those who can quote it backward and forward: We all need waves and waves of God's grace to get through this life.

Over the next 40 days, we're going to set sail on an adventure with Jonah. At times it will seem like a *mis*adventure. Jonah gets himself into one messy situation after another, yet God continues to love him through it all. By seeing how God loved Jonah in the middle of his mess, we can be confident that God loves us in the middle of ours.

Take some time to read the book of Jonah today. It's only four chapters with a total of 48 verses and can be read in about ten minutes. As you read, try to approach the story with fresh eyes, as if you've never heard of Jonah (or the big fish) before.

As we explore this book together, we'll discover that, just as *E.T.* is not about bicycles, the story of Jonah is not about a fish.

It's a story about how God doesn't want anyone left out and the depths he'll go to remind us of that beautiful truth.

> **Questions to Ponder:**
>
> What has your experience been with the story of Jonah?
>
> After reading the entire book of Jonah, what would you say the story is about? Write down anything about the story that stuck out to you this time around.

Day 2:
But Did It Really Happen?

Today's Bible Reading: Matthew 12:38-42

Before we dive into *(pun intended!)* our adventure with Jonah, I want to spend a few days looking at some background information on the book. Yesterday, we looked at how Jonah's story is more than a simple fish tale. Even so, the question remains: Is the story fact or fiction, history or fable?

Believe it or not, biblical scholars are divided on this issue. It's not simply a case of, "If you take the Bible seriously, then you believe the story of Jonah is true." The Bible is a library of 66 different books. If we want to take the Bible seriously, we need to understand the literary genre of each individual book. While opinions on the book of Jonah vary, they fall into one of two general categories.

1. Jonah as Historical Narrative

In this view, the story of Jonah is taken as history. Everything in the story happened as written. There are several reasons why this view is reasonable.

First, Jonah was a real person mentioned in the historical book of 2 Kings. We'll take a closer look at who he was in a few days.

Second, Nineveh was a real city in Assyria, and their brutality is well-documented. We'll talk more about their vile reputation as we get into the story.

Finally, Jesus himself spoke about Jonah and Nineveh. In Matthew 12, some Pharisees ask Jesus to show them a "sign" that he is the Messiah. Jesus responds to their request with these words:

But Jesus replied, "Only an evil, adulterous generation would demand a miraculous sign; but the only sign I will give them is the sign of the prophet Jonah. For as Jonah was in the belly of the great fish for three days and three nights, so will the Son of Man be in the heart of the earth for three days and three nights. (Matthew 12:39–40, NLT)

By referencing Jonah's journey to the belly of a fish and back, Jesus was foreshadowing his own journey to the grave and back.

2. Jonah as Historical Parable

Some commentators believe Jonah fits into the "historical parable" category. They don't deny Jonah was a real person who worked as a prophet of God. But they believe this historical figure was chosen to be the lead character of a *fictional* story. And, like Jesus' parables, the story was created to share a truth about God.

The argument for this view is *not* that it's impossible for a man to survive inside a fish for three days. We know that with God, all things are possible. *(Once again, we have to set the fish free for a moment!)* Instead, supporters of this view say the book of Jonah reads like satire. Tim Mackie of The Bible Project points out that satires often put well-known figures in extreme circumstances and use humor to critique character flaws.[1] Jonah was famous for prophesying the downfall of Israel's enemies. He'd be a comical choice to put at the center of a story about God's love for these same people!

So, where do I land on this debate? I lean toward option one, but I also leave room for some creative storytelling.

---

1 BibleProject. "Overview: Jonah." YouTube, 12 Apr. 2016, https://www.youtube.com/watch?v=dLIabZc0O4c.

DAY 2: BUT DID IT REALLY HAPPEN?

I believe Jonah's story is historical and unfolded as written. (I'll tell you my number one reason for believing this toward the end of our journey!) But I also believe the author played up the irony and humor of this story to get his point across. He was a master storyteller who knew what he was doing. Throughout the story, the author takes every opportunity to portray Jonah as a stumbling buffoon. And because of that, the reader is forced to wrestle with their own brokenness.

No matter where we land, I think it's important to respect others who have a different view. It's possible for people who share a deep reverence for the Bible to come to different conclusions.

Whether it's seen as history, parable, or something in between, one thing is certain: Jonah's story gives us a clear picture of God's love for messy, broken people (like me).

> ### 💬 Questions to Ponder:
>
> What do you think of the two views of the book of Jonah? Do you think it's possible to respect others who share a view different from the one you hold?
>
> Where do you land on the question, "But did it really happen?" How did you come to that conclusion?

Day 3:
It's All About You

Today's Bible Reading: Jonah 4

Sometimes it's hard to understand how Bible stories connect to our everyday lives. And some stories—like Jonah—are so familiar to us that we read them with a sense of detachment. We know what's coming (or *think* we know) and switch to autopilot mode without realizing it.

One way to see familiar stories in fresh ways is to put ourselves in the center of the action. So as we begin our journey, I want us to keep an idea in mind: This story is all about *you*.

Throughout our adventure, we're going to see Jonah make some poor choices. When God tells him to go to Nineveh, Jonah runs away because he's afraid that God might have the audacity to forgive the Ninevites. And when Jonah's worst nightmare comes true, he gives God a sarcastic, "I told you so!" response.

When we get to the end of the book, it can be easy to shake our heads and say, "Wow. That Jonah guy just doesn't get it." But if we do, we miss what the story is trying to tell us about *ourselves*. The truth is, there's a little Jonah in all of us just waiting to take control of the ship!

Jonah is a complex character. At first, his reasons for doing what he does seem straightforward. But when we dig deeper, we see that he struggles with the same things we do. Is Jonah a good guy or a bad guy? As with most Bible characters, the answer isn't so clear cut. Jonah is a messy, broken human who is loved by God, just as we are.

The more I read this book, the more I realize how much I have in common with Jonah. It's an uncomfortable feeling. I am so quick to write people off because they don't "get it" (whatever "it" happens to be) the way I do. There's always a group of people I can point a finger at to give myself a sense of moral superiority.

A few days ago, my wife and I got into a small argument. (I prefer to call it a kerfuffle.) I felt like she wasn't as compassionate as I was about a topic we were discussing. Soon, I felt my head begin to swell with pride. *I am so caring!* I thought. A few moments later, I felt God tenderly tap me on the shoulder, as he did with Jonah. I went back to my wife and said, "I'm sorry. I'm being a Jonah." (In case you're wondering, she graciously forgave me.)

Some early Christian commentators used the book of Jonah to give life to antisemitic ideas.[2] By judging Jonah (who was Jewish), they argued Christians were superior to Jews. We must be careful to not go down that dangerous road. If we're using Jonah's story to judge other people (as I've been guilty of), then we're overlooking the whole point.

The book of Jonah ends with God asking Jonah a question:

Then the LORD said, "You feel sorry about the plant, though you did nothing to put it there. It came quickly and died quickly. But Nineveh has more than 120,000 people living in spiritual darkness, not to mention all the animals. **Shouldn't I feel sorry for such a great city?"** (Jonah 4:10–11, NLT, emphasis mine)

We never hear Jonah's response. Did the author end the book too soon? No, he ended it at the perfect spot! Because as you close the book, you come to a stunning realization about God's unanswered question: *It's all about you.*

---

2 Yanklowitz, Shmuly. "Introduction." *The Book of Jonah: A Social Justice Commentary*, Central Conference of American Rabbis, New York, 2020, p. xx.

> 💬 **Questions to Ponder:**
>
> In what ways are you like Jonah? In what ways are you different from Jonah?
>
> Are there any groups of people you are tempted to judge because they just "don't get it"?
>
> How would you respond to God's final question to Jonah?

Day 4:
Jonah on The Tonight Show

Today's Bible Reading: 2 Kings 14:23-29

We've spent the past three days looking at the book of Jonah as a whole. Yesterday, we considered why we shouldn't be too hard on good ol' Jonah. (*Fair warning:* We're still going to have some fun exploring Jonah's comic foibles. Remember, the author was intentional about drawing out the humor in this story. But the purpose will always be to see what Jonah's actions reveal about *us*.) Tomorrow we'll start walking through the story chronologically. But since we're going to be spending the next few weeks with Jonah, let's get to know him a bit more.

Jonah was a prophet in Israel sometime in the eighth century B.C. His background is briefly mentioned in the book of 2 Kings. The story goes like this:

After the reign of Solomon—King David's son—there was a rift over who should be Israel's next king. It got so bad that the nation divided itself into two kingdoms. The northern kingdom kept the name Israel while the southern kingdom went by the name Judah. Both kingdoms had their fair share of evil kings, but Israel had some whoppers.

One of these kings was Jeroboam II. Despite being a bad king, God had some good news for him. Over the years, Assyria had invaded Israel and taken over its land. And they weren't very friendly neighbors. Assyria knew all sorts of creative ways to inflict physical and psychological torture on its enemies. But then, God allowed King

Jeroboam II to recover those stolen territories. And who do you think God tapped to deliver that message? Our friend Jonah!

Jonah's message of victory gave hope to his country. I'm sure he became a national hero and made the rounds on all the popular talk shows (imagine Jimmy Fallon interviewing Jonah!). Israel had been oppressed by their enemies for far too long. Assyria was finally going to get what they had coming to them. God himself spoke this promise through Jonah.

And then, some time later (maybe as Jonah is still opening his fan mail), God calls on Jonah again. He has another message about Assyria. But this time, God wants Jonah to pack his bags and head to Nineveh, the capital city. This isn't quite the vacation Jonah was hoping for! Old Testament scholar John Goldingay sums up the irony of Jonah's backstory:

The reason for telling this story about Jonah is that a prophet who gave such a positive promise to [Israel] is the last kind of person to enthuse over Nineveh escaping God's judgment.[3]

And so, as the curtain rises on our story, Jonah—everyone's favorite prophet—is being sent by God into enemy territory.

Now, what could possibly go wrong?

 Questions to Ponder:

Does knowing more about Jonah's background help you see his story in a new way?

What emotions may have bubbled up in Jonah when God told him to go to Nineveh? Can you relate to these feelings at all?

---

3   Goldingay, John. *Daniel and the Twelve Prophets for Everyone*. Westminster John Knox Press, 2016.

Day 5:
Sending Nineveh a Peace Offering

Today's Bible Reading: Jonah 1:1-3
Supporting Passage: Genesis 8

The LORD gave this message to Jonah son of Amittai: "Get up and go to the great city of Nineveh. Announce my judgment against it because I have seen how wicked its people are." But Jonah got up and went in the opposite direction to get away from the LORD.

Today, we officially set sail on our adventure with Jonah! We'll be looking at the story one small section at a time and pondering what it means for us.

We've already learned that Jonah was a prophet who delivered messages from God. There are many prophets in the Bible, and we don't know how God chose to communicate to each one. It could have been through dreams, visions, or even an audible voice. In 1 Kings 19, God speaks to the prophet Elijah through a gentle whisper. No matter the method, the book of Jonah opens with God communicating a message to our hero loud and clear: *Go to Nineveh*. And upon receiving it, Jonah takes off in the opposite direction. Exciting start!

This brings us to our first question. Why did Jonah run?

Some people think Jonah was afraid of going to Nineveh. The Ninevites had a nasty reputation for cruelty. I've read some pretty gruesome descriptions of how good the Ninevites were at torture. I hesitate to repeat them here because I don't want either of us to have nightmares! But I'll let author Skye Jethani give us a little peek into the terror:

[Archeologists] have unearthed writings from Nineveh that chronicle the city's atrocities. One Ninevite king built "a pyramid of heads" in front of a city he'd sacked and boasted that "their youths and their women I burnt up in the flames." Another king had his enemy flayed and his skin displayed on the city wall.[4]

Since Assyria occupied part of Israel for a time, the Ninevites may have even killed some of Jonah's friends and family. So, I can't argue that the thought of walking straight into Torture Town probably filled Jonah with fear. But that's not the *main* reason why he refused to do what God asked. In Jonah 4, Jonah confesses the real reason why he ran:

"Didn't I say before I left home that you would do this, LORD? **That is why I ran away to Tarshish! I knew that you are a merciful and compassionate God, slow to get angry and filled with unfailing love.** You are eager to turn back from destroying people." (Jonah 4:2, NLT, emphasis mine)

At first glance, Jonah's reasoning doesn't seem to add up. After all, God told Jonah to "Announce my *judgment* against [Nineveh]." Wouldn't Jonah be gleeful to deliver such a gloomy message to his enemies? The problem was, Jonah knew God too well. He couldn't trust God to stick to the plan!

The name Jonah means "dove" in Hebrew.[5] And doves represent peace throughout the Bible. After God flooded the earth, Noah released a dove from the ark. When it didn't return, Noah knew the flood was over. It was safe to come out and start a new life with his family.

I don't know if Jonah had that story in his mind when he ran from

---

4   Jethani, Skye. "Who Is the Moral Monster?" With God Daily, 30 June 2021.
5   Zaklikowski, Chana Raizel. "What Does the Name Jonah Mean?" Chabad.org, https://www.chabad.org/library/article_cdo/aid/1702445/jewish/What-Does-the-Name-Jonah-Mean.htm.

DAY 5: SENDING NINEVEH A PEACE OFFERING

God. Maybe he sensed God was sending him to Nineveh as a peace offering. And he wanted no part of it.

Jonah was right about one thing: The Ninevites *did* deserve God's judgment. They had done unspeakable things, bringing terror, pain, and destruction wherever they went.

But so do we. We may not be building a pyramid of heads in our backyard (if you are, please stop), but we're still a mess. The trouble is, there will always be a "Nineveh" out there to compare ourselves to. Next to them, we look pretty good. By keeping the focus on all the Ninevehs of this world, we ignore the brokenness inside ourselves.

But the good news is, God sent us a dove as well. Centuries later, God became one of us. Jesus entered into our mess. And when he was baptized, the Holy Spirit descended on him "like a dove" (Matthew 3:16).

Jonah begrudgingly became God's peace offering to one city. But Jesus—the greater Jonah—became God's peace offering to the entire world. And he did it because he doesn't want anyone left out.

 Questions to Ponder:

Why do you think Jonah ran from God?

How has God made peace with you? Is God asking you to bring his peace to anyone this week?

Day 6:
Setting off for a Distant Country

Today's Bible Reading: Jonah 1:1-3
Supporting Passage: Luke 15:11-32

The LORD gave [a] message to Jonah son of Amittai... But Jonah... went down to the port of Joppa, where he found a ship leaving for Tarshish. He bought a ticket and went on board, hoping to escape from the LORD by sailing to Tarshish.

At the start of Jonah's story, we learn that the message he received came from "the LORD." This is the personal name of Israel's God, also known as YHWH. It was the name God revealed to Moses on Mount Sinai when he referred to himself as, "The LORD, the LORD, the compassionate and gracious God, slow to anger, abounding in love and faithfulness" (Exodus 34:6, NIV).

Jonah had a lot of knowledge about God. (Later, in chapter four, he even attempts to use this knowledge to win an argument.) But despite *knowing* all the right things, Jonah still ran away when God asked him to go to Nineveh. And it wasn't a minor detour, either. Jonah wanted to get as far away from Nineveh as humanly possible!

Nineveh was about 500 miles east of Israel, located in modern-day Iraq. Jonah took off to Tarshish, which was 2000 miles west of Israel on the southern coast of Spain. That would be like God asking someone in Atlanta to go to Richmond, Virginia, and instead, they high tail it to Los Angeles!

Did Jonah really think God wouldn't find him if he left town? This

DAY 6: SETTING OFF FOR A DISTANT COUNTRY

seems unlikely, given how much knowledge Jonah had about God. Other ancient gods may have been confined to a location, but Jonah knew YHWH wasn't. By fleeing to Tarshish, I think Jonah was engaging in a bit of theatrics. He was making a dramatic point and telling God, "This is how wrong you are about this little job you have for me!" A prophet of God so blatantly disobeying his call is one of the many ironic elements we'll see in this book.

There are several parallels between Jonah's story and Jesus' parable of the prodigal son. (That's our supporting passage for today, and we'll be referring back to it throughout this journey.) In that story, the younger brother takes his father's money and "sets off for a distant country" (Luke 15:11, NIV). By cashing out his inheritance, he was essentially telling his father, "You're dead to me!"

Some commentators believe Jonah chartered the entire ship to take him to Tarshish.[6] If so, it would have cost him a pretty penny. And even if he didn't reserve the whole boat, he'd still need a significant amount of money to fund his getaway trip. *(Maybe he had a nice nest egg built up from all those publicity appearances!)* Both Jonah and the younger brother used their wealth to escape to a distant country.

Money has the capacity to do a tremendous amount of good. But it can also make it easier for us to avoid doing what God calls us to do. Like Jonah, we know we can't *literally* run from God. But, if we're not careful, money can insulate us from the world. If things start feeling a little too uncomfortable, there's always an escape hatch. Money can keep us preoccupied but the comforts it provides are temporary. The younger brother discovered this unpleasant truth when his bank balance hit zero.

I don't say this to make you feel guilty. Money is a topic that can stir up feelings of shame in everyone, no matter which tax bracket we

---

6   H. Wolff, *Obadiah and Jonah* (Minneapolis: Augsburg, 1986), 102

find ourselves in. But with Jesus, there's no need for shame because he's in the mess with us. As Jonah set sail in the opposite direction of Nineveh, God loved him. And as the younger brother walked away from his father, bagfuls of cash in hand, his father was already planning an epic welcome home party for him.

There's no distant country we can go to that's too distant for God's grace to reach us.

 Questions to Ponder:

Why is it still so easy to run from God even when we have the correct knowledge about him?

What similarities do you see between Jonah and the younger brother?

Has money ever made it easier for you to run from God? Take some time to remember that God's love and grace can reach you wherever you find yourself today.

Day 7:
"Please Send Someone Else!"

Today's Bible Reading: Jonah 1:1-3
Supporting Passage: Exodus 3:1-4:17

[Jonah] bought a ticket and went on board, hoping to escape from the LORD by sailing to Tarshish.

Let's flex our creative muscles a bit. If you read the above verse without knowing the rest of Jonah's story, what would you expect to happen next? Maybe something like this:

And so the LORD chose a different prophet to go to Nineveh—someone who actually cared about the Ninevites. And this prophet obeyed God, and everyone lived happily ever after. (Except for disobedient Jonah, who no one ever heard from again. Good riddance!)

Jonah's story *should* have ended when he boarded the ship to Tarshish. God didn't need Jonah. He could've called on the next prophet in line. He could've said, "Okay, Jonah, the train (or boat) is leaving with or without you on it. Plenty of other people would love to have this job!"

But yet, Jonah's story continues after verse 3.

Sometimes it seems like God relishes choosing the worst person for a given job. And when that person tries to wiggle their way out of it, God refuses to pass them over for a better candidate. We see this over and over in the Bible. Why does God create headaches for himself?

Humans like to see immediate results. When there's a job to be done, we look to give it to the most qualified individual. We want the project completed on time and under budget. But when God calls us to do a job, his primary concern isn't efficiency. It's about changing *us* in the process. One of my favorite examples of this principle is when God calls on Moses to lead the Israelites out of Egypt.

In Exodus 3, God appears to Moses in a burning bush and tells him to confront Pharaoh. Moses tries to talk his way out of the job five times. He deflects, he stalls, and he makes excuses. He points out his own weakness as a way to disqualify himself:

"O Lord, I'm not very good with words… I get tongue-tied, and my words get tangled." (Exodus 4:10, NLT)

It turns out God is aware of Moses' shortcomings but wants him for the job anyway. And when Moses sees his options fading, he makes one last effort to duck out by delivering one of the most relatable lines in the Bible:

But Moses again pleaded, "Lord, please! Send anyone else." (Exodus 4:13, NLT)

Moses is gripped by terror and self-doubt, and God can see this. So God allows Moses to bring along his brother Aaron to help him. Imagine that! God promises Moses that he would be with him, but Moses still needs the support of another person. I think it's beautiful that God obliges Moses in this way.

Moses and Jonah had different reasons for trying to avoid what God asked them to do. But their stories—like so many other stories—didn't end when they said "no." God kept pursuing them, even when it didn't make sense from a human perspective.

When God asks us to do something, we may feel like we're the worst person in the world for the job. We may repeat Moses' desperate cry of "Send someone else!" But the reason we have for avoiding the job might be the reason *why* God is choosing us. Maybe Jonah was the person who needed to go to Nineveh the most. There's more to serving God than getting things done efficiently. He uses our imperfect acts of service to do a work *in us*.

God used Nineveh to change Jonah's heart. What will he use to change yours?

 Questions to Ponder:

Is God asking you to do anything that you feel unwilling or unqualified to do? How is God pursuing you despite your pleas to, "Send someone else!"

Has God ever put an "Aaron" in your life—someone who supported you when God asked you to do something scary? Is there anyone you can be an Aaron to this week?

Day 8:
Compassion in the Storm

Today's Bible Reading: Jonah 1:4-6
Supporting Passage: Mark 4:35-41

[T]he Lord hurled a powerful wind over the sea, causing a violent storm that threatened to break the ship apart… But all this time Jonah was sound asleep down in the hold.

We've already discussed how the author of Jonah is a master storyteller. He portrays everything in the story as larger than life. Inanimate objects take on a personality of their own, including the ship caught in the storm. In the original Hebrew, verse 4 might be translated as, "The ship was *determined* to break apart."[7]

Despite the ship (and its crew) being in distress, this terrible storm didn't appear to phase Jonah. He was downstairs in the lounge catching some Zs.

When I read this part of the story, I can't help but think of a similar story found in the New Testament: the time when Jesus calmed the storm. (That's our supporting passage for today.) Both Jesus and Jonah were caught in a violent storm while on a boat. Both were asleep. And both were woken up by people who couldn't believe they could nap at a time like this. But while Jesus' sleep was a restful one, Jonah's sleep was full of despair.

---

7   Smith, Billy K., and Frank S. Page. *Amos, Obadiah, Jonah*, Broadman & Holman, Nashville Ten., 1995, p. 229.

DAY 8: COMPASSION IN THE STORM

We're not told why Jonah was asleep. Exhaustion may have caught up to him after planning his last-minute trip to Tarshish. But I also think he was filled with a sense of hopelessness. Jonah had "gone below deck" (1:5, NIV). He wasn't in a chatty mood. If Jonah had taken an Uber to Tarshish, he would have sat in the backseat and put in his AirPods. There'd be no small talk on the ride.

I imagine Jonah fell into the kind of dreadful sleep that leaves you feeling more tired when you wake up. It's a sleep many of us have experienced. The struggles of life can lead us into dark places. For some, the cloud of hopelessness may only last a season. But for others, depression is an ongoing reality.

According to one source, depression affects about 17.3 million Americans per year.[8] And as much as we might like it to be the case, followers of Jesus are not immune. You can love Jesus deeply and also battle feelings of despair. I know because I've experienced it firsthand.

I've had days when it was a struggle to get out of bed. Sometimes it was due to external circumstances brought on by my own choices. Shame and guilt suffocated me, and I questioned whether God still loved me. But other times, there was no clear reason for my turmoil. I just couldn't face the day. These times have never lasted too long for me, but I know that for many, the struggle is daily.

Depression can be lonely, especially when you feel like no one understands how you feel. In a genuine effort to help, Christians can sometimes brush off the suffering of others. We say things like, "Cheer up, God loves you!" or, "Just give it to God." These phrases are meant to bring comfort. But they often do the opposite by dismissing the real pain someone is experiencing. It reminds me of one of my favorite proverbs:

---

8 "Depression Statistics." *Depression and Bipolar Support Alliance*, 12 July 2019, https://www.dbsalliance.org/education/depression/statistics/.

*Singing light songs to the heavyhearted
is like pouring salt in their wounds.* (Proverbs 25:20, MSG)

If you find yourself in a battle with depression, please tell someone. Yes, God is with you and will never leave you. But God also created us to live in community so that we don't have to walk through our storms alone. Seeking help from others—whether a counselor, medical professional, or trusted friend—isn't a lack of faith. It's a sign of being fully human.

And when we have loved ones facing depression, let's allow compassion to lead the way. It's tempting to want to bring our suffering friend "above deck" to sing happy songs. But sometimes, the best thing we can do is go below deck to where they are and hold their hand until the storm passes.

> 💬 Questions to Ponder:
>
> What similarities do you see between the stories of Jesus calming the storm and Jonah? What differences do you see?
>
> Have you ever experienced the kind of sleep that leaves you feeling more tired when you wake up?
>
> If you are currently struggling with depression, what is one step you can take to seek help? If you know someone struggling, how can you show them compassion?

Day 9:
Waves of Grace

Today's Bible Reading: Jonah 1:4-6

[T]he LORD hurled a powerful wind over the sea, causing a violent storm that threatened to break the ship apart.

The word "sin" carries a lot of baggage. For Christians, it can trigger feelings of guilt, shame, and never being good enough. I remember times as a teenager, sitting in church and wondering if I was ever going to get my act together. And for people who are not Christians, the word can seem outdated and judgemental.

But maybe we are overcomplicating it. One of my favorite definitions of *sin* is that it's simply anything you do that breaks the peace you have with God, others, or yourself. And Jonah—whose name symbolizes peace—broke it with all three when he boarded the ship to Tarshish.

Jonah broke the peace he had with God by doing the opposite of what God told him to do. He broke the peace he had with others by not extending compassion to the Ninevites. And, judging by his attitude on the ship, Jonah lost a sense of inner peace. It was at that moment when a storm started brewing.

The story makes it clear that God caused the storm. Verse four says God "*hurled*" a powerful wind over the sea." In other places in the Bible, that same word describes hurling a spear,[9] which is a pretty cool image! But was God hurling this spear-shaped gust of wind to

---
9 Smith, p. 229.

punish Jonah? Some may make that argument. I think the answer is a lot more nuanced.

As we've already discussed, Jonah seemed like the worst person to send to Nineveh. (If Jonah's high school gave out superlatives, he would have won the "Least Likely To Go To Nineveh" Award.) But Jonah didn't know the whole story. God had something planned for Jonah that he could only reveal inside the walls of Nineveh. In Nineveh, God was going to give Jonah a deeper understanding of his love. God's grace was found *in* the storm.

But not all of life's storms are created equal. I think there are at least three different kinds of storms we can find ourselves in.

Some storms brew up from the natural consequences of our actions. God didn't create arbitrary rules so that he could punish us when we break them. God's law has a purpose. As author J. Ellsworth Kalas puts it, the commandments of God "help us live better, and they make us better to live with."[10] If we sin against others (AKA, break the peace we have with them) or make unwise choices for our lives (AKA, break the peace we have with ourselves), we may suffer from the natural consequences of our actions.

When we find ourselves in these kinds of storms, there's grace from God to seek forgiveness and restore the peace we've lost.

Then there are the storms blown in from living in a messy world. If you are suffering through an illness or some other tragedy, you may drop to your knees and say, *Why, God? What have I done to deserve this?!* I want you to know you've done nothing to deserve it. God is not punishing you. This broken world is groaning for redemption just as we are. (Romans 8:22)

---

10   Kalas, J. Ellsworth. *Grace in a Tree Stump: Old Testament Stories of God's Love.* Westminster John Knox Press, 2005.

When we find ourselves in these kinds of storms, there's grace from God to receive comfort. Jesus came into this world to walk *with you* through times of suffering. He loves you.

And, every now and then, we find ourselves in a "Jonah" storm. We are running from the work God wants to do in us, and he is trying to bring us back. When God hurled that wind toward the ship, he wasn't saying, "Take that, Jonah! This is what you get for disobeying me!" He was saying, "Jonah. I need you to come back. There's a purpose in all this mess, and you won't understand it until we get to Nineveh. I love you too much to leave you behind."

When we find ourselves in these kinds of storms, there's grace from God to turn the ship around and head to Nineveh.

No matter what kind of storm we're in, God provides us with waves and waves of grace.

 Questions to Ponder:

What do you think of the idea that sin is "anything you do that breaks the peace you have with God, others, or yourself"? How have you seen sin break the peace you have with those three things?

Are you caught in a storm right now? If so, what kind is it? How is God providing you with grace in the storm?

Day 10:
"How Can You Sleep at a Time Like This?"

Today's Bible Reading: Jonah 1:4-6

Fearing for their lives, the desperate sailors shouted to their gods for help and threw the cargo overboard to lighten the ship. But all this time Jonah was sound asleep down in the hold. So the captain went down after him. "How can you sleep at a time like this?" he shouted. "Get up and pray to your god!"

Yesterday, we saw how God hurled a storm at Jonah to bring him back from his getaway mission. But Jonah wasn't the only person aboard the ship. The sailors inadvertently got caught in Jonah's mess. This is a reminder that the storms of life are not self-contained. We sometimes get caught up in the storms of others, as they get caught up in ours.

The crew in charge of the ship are interesting characters. They were probably Phonencians—skilled sailors who navigated the Mediterranean Sea. They worshiped a multitude of ancient gods. Each god was in charge of something different, so they wanted to cover all their bases. (Kind of like throwing spaghetti at the wall and seeing what sticks.) Like the Ninevites, they were "outsiders" to Jonah's religion. And there was something deeply ironic about Jonah being stuck in a storm with them. Tim Keller points out, "[Jonah] did not want to talk to pagans about God… So he fled—only to find himself talking to the exact sort of people he was fleeing!"[11]

These sailors were not novices when it came to navigating a ship

---

11   Keller, Timothy. *The Prodigal Prophet: Jonah and the Mystery of God's Mercy*, Penguin Random House, New York, 2018, pp. 32–33.

through bad weather. And yet, even they were terrified by the storm. Maybe they sensed there was something different about this one. So they start throwing up prayers to the various gods to see if anything will work. But the storm continues to rage. And that's when the captain of the ship goes below deck and shakes Jonah awake. (By the way, the word for *captain* literally means "head of the rope pullers."[12] I don't have any profound takeaway on that one. I just thought it was funny.)

So the captain went down after him. "How can you sleep at a time like this?" he shouted. "Get up and pray to your god! Maybe he will pay attention to us and spare our lives." (Jonah 1:6, NLT)

It's remarkable that this captain—a man who has no understanding of the true God—has to wake up a prophet of God to pray. He doesn't understand how anyone can sleep when there is so much terror going on outside. This is a challenging message to all Christians.

Followers of Jesus should be a force for good in this world. Jesus said to "let your good deeds shine out for all to see, so that everyone will praise your heavenly Father" (Matthew 5:16, NLT). But too often, non-Christians are baffled by our apathy toward the world's injustices. They don't understand why we don't seem to care about issues like poverty, racism, and abuse.

I think part of the problem is our tendency to put all the focus on heaven. We view the world as Jonah's sinking ship. Instead of pitching in to help, we say, "Don't worry! Everything will be great once we get to heaven! We just have to grin and bear it until Jesus comes back to take us away." But Jesus promised to bring his beautiful kingdom *to earth*. We get to join him in that process now, with the knowledge that it won't be fully completed until his return. This is what the early church did, and the world took notice. They loved and cared for society's most vulnerable—those inside the church *and* in the broader community.

---

12 Smith, p. 231.

Once Jonah wakes up, there's no indication that he does anything to try to help the situation. The sailors, however, are doing everything they can. They are throwing precious cargo overboard while Jonah silently watches.

As I said, this is a challenging message and one I need to hear more than anyone. I know there are areas of my life where apathy has set in. I've been woken up by non-Christians who are making a positive difference in this world. They wonder how I could be sleeping at a time like this. I wonder, too.

But like everything in Jonah's story, there is grace. There is forgiveness for the times we've fallen asleep. And there is grace to wake up and join in the work.

 Questions to Ponder:

Have you ever been caught up in someone else's storm? Has anyone ever been caught up in yours? How did you see God's grace in the situation?

Have you ever been "woken up" by a non-Christian about an issue facing the world? If so, how did you respond?

Day 11:
Kindness & Patience in the Storm

Today's Bible Reading: Jonah 1:7-13
Supporting Passages: Acts 1:12-26; Galatians 5:16-26

"Throw me into the sea," Jonah said, "and it will become calm again. I know that this terrible storm is all my fault." Instead, the sailors rowed even harder to get the ship to the land.

Yesterday, we took a closer look at the sailors who got caught in Jonah's storm. These men were polytheists who did not know the true God. Despite this, they sprung into action when danger struck, while Jonah shrugged his shoulders.

After the captain wakes Jonah up, the sailors cast lots to see who made the gods angry. Casting lots is similar to rolling dice or drawing straws, and it was a common practice in the Old Testament. There was nothing "magical" about the lots themselves. But God sometimes worked through them to reveal his will. (Interestingly, the final time we see lots used in the Bible is in Acts 1. The disciples had to choose a replacement for Judas, and they employ this method to make the decision. In the next chapter, Jesus sends the Holy Spirit to guide and comfort each believer. *No dice required!*)

Jonah draws the short straw, and all eyes turn to him. The sailors know who's to blame for the storm. They could throw Jonah overboard right now and be done with this mess. But instead, they show patience. They question Jonah to gather more information about the situation. They discover that he is on the run from "the God of heaven, who made the sea and the land" (Jonah 1:9, NLT). Yikes!

The sailors are perplexed about why Jonah would do such a thing. But despite being terrified, they resist forming an angry mob. Instead, they ask Jonah what they should do, and he gives this answer:

"Throw me into the sea," Jonah said, "and it will become calm again. I know that this terrible storm is all my fault." (Jonah 1:12, NLT)

Commentators are divided over Jonah's motives here. Was he sorry for his actions that put these men in danger? Or was he looking for the ultimate way out of going to Nineveh?

As I said at the beginning of this adventure, Jonah is a complex character. He's a messy human, which means his motives can be all over the place. As a storm rages outside, there's a bigger one churning inside of Jonah. I can relate.

I think when Jonah looked into the sailors' terrified faces, he realized the gravity of what he had done. He doesn't want anyone to get hurt, so he takes responsibility for his actions. He's willing to sacrifice himself for their safety.

At the same time, notice what Jonah *doesn't* say. He doesn't say, "Turn the ship around and head to Nineveh, and the sea will become calm again." Why is Jonah still avoiding Nineveh?

Maybe Jonah thought it was too late for second chances, and a watery grave was what he deserved. I've experienced that kind of debilitating guilt before. Maybe Jonah was sliding further and further down into hopelessness. Or maybe Jonah was still so against going to Nineveh that he'd rather be dead. No matter his motives, his despair at this moment is real.

But the sailors are a ray of hope in the storm. For the third time, they choose kindness when it would have been easier to make a knee-jerk reaction. They try their best to row back to safety instead of immediately throwing Jonah overboard. Once again, the "outsiders" are teaching us lessons.

It can be so easy to form a mob to go after those we think are guilty. We may not grab pitchforks and torches, but we are quick to launch unkind words and accusations. But here, the sailors show patience. They try to understand the situation before jumping into action. And even when Jonah's guilt was clear, their desire wasn't to pay him back for what he'd done.

It's a reminder to let kindness and patience guide our actions, even in the chaos of a storm. And that is something we desperately need the Holy Spirit's help to do. *(No dice required!)*

 Questions to Ponder:

Why do you think Jonah told the sailors to throw him overboard? Can you relate to any of his possible motives?

What are some ways mob mentality displays itself in today's culture? *(If you're having trouble thinking of examples, start by considering the influence of social media.)* How can you—with the Holy Spirit's help—let kindness and patience lead the way in these times?

Day 12:
Religious Man Overboard!

Today's Bible Reading: Jonah 1:13-16
Supporting Passage: Romans 12:9-21

Then the sailors picked Jonah up and threw him into the raging sea, and the storm stopped at once! The sailors were awestruck by the LORD's great power, and they offered him a sacrifice and vowed to serve him.

Today we are wrapping up the first major section of the book of Jonah: Jonah's big sea adventure with the sailors. We saw these sailors refuse to harm Jonah even though he was responsible for the raging storm. Rather than toss him into the sea, they try their best to navigate back to land. But it's no use. The sea grows wilder. So now, with options waning, the sailors give into Jonah's request to throw him overboard. But first, they cry out to Jonah's God for mercy:

Then they cried out to the LORD, "Please, LORD, do not let us die for taking this man's life. Do not hold us accountable for killing an innocent man, for you, LORD, have done as you pleased." Then they took Jonah and threw him overboard, and the raging sea grew calm. (Jonah 1:14–15, NIV)

A splash is heard as Jonah hits the water. And then, in an instant, the dark clouds part, letting in the sunshine. Gentle laps of water replace the violent waves. Birds chirp a happy tune. All is calm.

The author of Jonah has painted an ironic picture for us. Think about it: These "pagan" sailors had to throw a religious man overboard for the sea to grow calm. It turns everything we'd expect from a Bible story

DAY 12: RELIGIOUS MAN OVERBOARD!

upside down. And, like most things in this story, it issues a challenge for those of us who follow God.

When we interact with the world, are we bringing God's peace to it? Or are we adding to the chaos? We are called to be peacemakers. The Apostle Paul says, "If it is possible, as far as it depends on you, live at peace with everyone" (Romans 12:18, NIV). In every conversation, we have a choice to sow seeds of either unity or division.

If you were to be "thrown overboard" from social media, would your corner of Facebook grow calm? What about the churches in our communities? If they all closed their doors tomorrow, would their presence be missed because of the positive impact they were making? Or would the neighborhood breathe a sigh of relief?

These are good questions to think about as we engage with the world. But the truth is, we're not going to get it right all the time. That's okay. God can use us to accomplish good, even when we mess up. He did it with Jonah. In a beautiful twist, God uses Jonah's defiance to change the sailors' lives:

The sailors were awestruck by the LORD's great power, and they offered him a sacrifice and vowed to serve him. (Jonah 1:16, NLT)

After their strange encounter with Jonah, these sailors vow to serve YHWH. There's a good chance this means they got off the ship, went to Jerusalem, and made a sacrifice at the temple. Imagine the priest's face when he saw a bunch of pagan sailors roll in from off the street!

This reminds me of an experience I had in college. I was in the musical *Cabaret*, and on opening night, I organized a pre-show prayer circle. I announced to the cast that we'd be praying backstage before the show. Anyone who wanted to join was welcome, but I wasn't expecting a huge turnout. I only knew of two or three other cast members who were Christians.

When I arrived backstage, I was shocked. Nearly half the cast was waiting to pray. As I looked around the circle, I kept thinking, "Huh… I didn't expect *her* to show up… Wow… *He* wants to pray?" Fifteen years later, I still think about that night. I was so quick to judge others. Like Jonah, I had already decided who was in and who was out. And I was embarrassingly wrong.

No one is out of God's reach. Not messy sailors, not mean Ninevites, and not judgy prophets. Not me. And not you.

The story of Jonah is a story about how God doesn't want anyone left out.

 Questions To Ponder:

In what situations are you most tempted to add to the division and chaos of this world? How can you be a peacemaker in the places where God has put you?

Take a moment to reread Jonah 1:1-16. What is one thing you've learned from this section of the story?

Day 13:
Sometimes Grace Smells Like Fish Guts

Today's Bible Reading: Jonah 1:17

Now the LORD provided a huge fish to swallow Jonah...

What is the "moral" of the book of Jonah? The answer, according to Christian pop culture, might sound something like this:

When God tells you to do something, you'd better do it... or else!

In this view, the fish is seen as payback for Jonah's disobedience. Jonah gets put in a "timeout" to sit and think about what he has done. While Jonah did get plenty of time to reflect inside the fish, it wasn't primarily a punishment. It was a gift of grace to save Jonah from death. (And as we begin to look at Jonah's prayer, we'll see that he viewed it from this perspective, too.)

The last verse of Jonah 1 says God "*provided* a huge fish to swallow Jonah." Other translations use the word *appointed*. God sent this fish on a rescue mission to save Jonah from the deadly waters. In the Bible, the sea is a symbol of chaos. (When Jesus sets all things right at the end of Revelation, John notes, "there was no longer any sea" [21:1, NIV].) As Jonah sank deeper and deeper into the chaos, a fish was flying through the water like a torpedo to provide him with a place of refuge.

As I imagine the fish swallowing Jonah whole, a funny thought crosses my mind. What if the fish acted like Jonah? What if the fish complained to God, "You can't be serious! You want me to show grace to *that guy*?! No way... I'm swimming in the opposite direction!" (I wonder, would

God then send a giant shark to swallow the big fish???) In another touch of irony, a fish follows God's instructions better than a prophet.

Now, I admit—being swallowed by a fish doesn't *seem* like a gift from God. It's not a place I would choose to be. But sometimes grace smells like fish guts. As Jonah floundered in the water, there was no way he could save himself. He couldn't clean up his own mess. And that is the best place to be in order to begin a process of healing.

Years ago, I found myself in a similar situation as Jonah. I had made a mess of life. I was swimming in the chaos of my own bad choices. And so, God provided me with a fish. (Don't worry—I wasn't literally swallowed by one!)

I joined a program at my church called reGROUP. It's a safe space where people can look at their stories and examine the broken places. It's a space to begin healing old wounds—both the wounds we have and the wounds we have given to others. (Other churches may have a similar ministry called Celebrate Recovery.) The process wasn't always pretty. It was painful at times, especially as I took an honest look at how my actions hurt others. But I was always met with grace by God and the reGROUP community.

The fish wasn't a punishment. It was a place of healing and hope. From inside the fish, Jonah finally remained still long enough for God to work on him. We all need places like that.

Not all fish look the same. Your "fish" might be a counselor's office or a program like Celebrate Recovery. It might be a choice to take a break from dating so you can give God space to heal old wounds. It might be reaching out to someone to ask for forgiveness. It might be a process of forgiving someone else. Whatever it is, the journey may be painful, but there is healing waiting on the other side. As Tim Keller says, "The usual place to learn the greatest secrets of God's grace is at the bottom."[13]

---

13 Keller, p. 73.

DAY 13: SOMETIMES GRACE SMELLS LIKE FISH GUTS

Sometimes grace smells like fish guts.

 Questions to Ponder:

Have you ever thought you were being punished by God, only to realize he was rescuing you?

Are you sinking in any sea of chaos right now? What "fish" might God be providing you?

If you'd like to find a Celebrate Recovery program near you, check out: CelebrateRecovery.com.

Day 14:
Making the Most of Your Time in a Fish

Today's Bible Reading: Jonah 1:17
Supporting Passage: Jeremiah 29:1-14

...and Jonah was in the belly of the fish three days and three nights.

Yesterday, we saw how God provided a huge fish to swallow Jonah. The belly of the sea creature wasn't a punishment but a place where God could begin working on Jonah's heart. Jonah spent three days and nights inside the fish. While three days may not seem like a long time, imagine what it must have felt like to be trapped down there. The utter darkness, the putrid smells, and the claustrophobia would become unbearable. Five minutes in this situation would feel like an eternity to me!

When God starts working in us, we often wish the process would move faster. As the saying goes, "God, give me patience, and give it to me *now*." But God is not concerned with speed. So when we find ourselves inside a "fish," we may as well settle in. The work could take a while.

Perhaps one of the most quoted verses in the Bible is Jeremiah 29:11:

"For I know the plans I have for you," declares the LORD, "plans to prosper you and not to harm you, plans to give you hope and a future." (NIV)

It's a hopeful verse found on coffee mugs, plaques, and couch pillows. It confirms that God has good plans for us. But the context of this promise often gets forgotten.

DAY 14: MAKING THE MOST OF YOUR TIME IN A FISH

After years of turning away from God, Jerusalem is conquered by Babylon. God's people are carried off from their homes and forced to live in this new land. In Jeremiah 29:11, God promises to bring his people back home... but only *after* a period of seventy years.

Seventy years?! That's like, a lifetime! No wonder that part gets left off of the coffee mug...

How were the people of Jerusalem supposed to bide their time until God came for them? God told them exactly how to spend their time in exile:

"Build homes, and plan to stay. Plant gardens, and eat the food they produce. Marry and have children. Then find spouses for them so that you may have many grandchildren... And work for the peace and prosperity of the city where I sent you into exile. Pray to the LORD for it, for its welfare will determine your welfare." (Jeremiah 29:5-7, NLT)

God didn't want his people to just wait around until they returned home. He wanted them to settle down and do good, even while in a place they didn't want to be. In other words, God wanted them to make the most of their time inside a fish.

It can be so tempting to want to hurry up and get to the next phase of life. We think, "Once I'm [insert blank], then I'll be happy." But maybe God is asking us to make the most of where we are right now. There is joy, purpose, and peace to be found in *this* moment.

Yesterday I talked about my time in reGROUP. When I first joined, I thought it would be a quick process. I was anxious to get through it so I could go back to life as usual. But as I started peeling back the layers of my story, I realized I was going to have to settle in for the long haul. I had to decide, *Am I going to be present here, or am I going to keep wishing I was somewhere else?* Full disclosure: I opted for the latter a lot more than I'd like to admit. But that's okay. When I felt trapped between the fish walls, my community helped me through it.

Jonah was in the belly of the fish for three days and nights. Outside, the world churned on without him. Nineveh still needed to be reached. But God wasn't in a hurry. Inside the fish, God used a hopeless place to give Jonah hope for the future.

When we find ourselves inside a fish, let's make the most of our time there.

 Questions to Ponder:

What do you think it was like for Jonah to be in the belly of a fish for three days?

Does knowing the context of Jeremiah 29:11 bring a new meaning to it? If so, how?

Are you hoping God will hurry up and bring you to a new stage of life? How can you settle in and make the most of where you're at right now?

Day 15:
Messy Prayer

Today's Bible Reading: Jonah 2:1
Supporting Passage: Romans 8:18-39

Then Jonah prayed to the LORD his God from inside the fish.

The second chapter of Jonah is where we get to the famous scene everyone knows: Jonah hanging out inside a fish. As we discussed back on day one, it has become the center of much debate, even among Christians. But if we make the fish the main focus, we miss what the chapter is *really* about. Chapter two is almost entirely a prayer Jonah prayed from the belly of the fish. So what does Jonah say to God? The answer isn't so simple, and some of it may surprise you.

Over the next few days, we'll unpack the prayer section by section and try to understand what Jonah is saying. But today, I want to focus on prayer in general.

I've always found Jonah's prayer a bit confusing. It's hard to decipher what he's saying. But then it hit me: *Jonah's prayer is messy.* And that's okay because all prayer is messy.

In his prayer, Jonah thanks God for rescuing him. And yet, he doesn't appear to say he's sorry for running away. In his prayer, Jonah promises to go to Nineveh. And yet, almost in the same breath, Jonah makes a backhanded dig at the Ninevites. Jonah's prayer seems altogether sincere *and* snarky. He's all over the place!

I am not criticizing Jonah. I admire him for choosing to talk to God after making such a mess of things. Jonah took the time to pray, and that's a big deal. So often, I am paralyzed by the thought of prayer. I know I should pray, but I imagine God as an impatient CEO rather than a loving father. If I don't approach him with the right words, then I'm wasting his time. He's looking at the clock, saying, "Get to the point, Murray, I've got more important things to do!" But the miracle of Jonah 2 is not that Jonah survived inside a fish. The miracle is that God listened to Jonah's messy, imperfect prayer.

Jonah's prayer reminds me that I can pray anytime, anywhere. Intellectually, I know this is true. But sometimes I have a hard time believing it. Sometimes I feel so far from God—so ashamed at where I find myself—that I think it's too late to turn to him. But those moments are the best times to pray because we can be the most honest with God. In the parable of the prodigal son, the younger brother "came to his senses" in a pigsty. And here, Jonah has been cast out into the abyss. These moments of hopelessness become ways of connecting with God.

But what happens when the despair is so overwhelming it crushes you? What happens when you can't open your mouth to utter a single prayer, even though you want to? God gave us a built-in failsafe! One of the most comforting verses to me is Romans 8:26:

In the same way, the Spirit helps us in our weakness. We do not know what we ought to pray for, but the Spirit himself intercedes for us through wordless groans. (NIV)

When we are too weak to pray, the Holy Spirit prays for us.

As we explore Jonah's prayer this week, let's remember that prayer is messy. Sometimes our desire to pray perfect prayers prevents us from praying at all. We might feel guilty for not praying the "right" way. We worry our motives are wrong. We beat ourselves up when our mind starts wandering mid-prayer. We doubt if our feeble, half-hearted attempt at prayer can do anything to heal the suffering in this world. Our prayers can seem so insignificant in the grand scheme of things.

But prayer isn't a formula to get right or a code to crack. It's about coming to God and being honest about how we're feeling. No matter how big of a mess we're in, it's never too late to pray. If Jonah could pray from the belly of a fish, then we can pray anywhere.

God hears and cares about every single messy, broken prayer.

 Questions to Ponder:

When you pray, do you imagine God more as an impatient CEO or a loving father? Why?

Do you find it difficult to pray? Are there times you worry about not praying the "right" way?

Would embracing "messy, imperfect prayers" change the way you pray? Take some time today to pray messy prayers. And if you're too weak to utter a word, take comfort in knowing the Spirit has you covered.

Day 16:
Anatomy of a Fish Prayer

Today's Bible Reading: Jonah 2:1-9

"In trouble, deep trouble, I prayed to God.
  He answered me."

Yesterday, we saw that messy people pray messy prayers. And that's okay because our prayers don't need to be perfect to reach God! Over the next few days, I want to break down Jonah's "fish prayer" and see what we can learn from it. We'll start today by looking at the prayer's basic structure. But first, a little disclaimer.

Prayer is an intimate moment between a human and God. Because it's a personal experience, it's generally not helpful to compare our prayer life to someone else's. If we wish we were more like *[insert "prayer warrior" here]*, we'll feel guilty that we're not praying enough. At the other end of the spectrum, if we criticize another person's prayers, pride will creep into our hearts. Since Jonah's prayer is included in this story, I think we're okay to poke at it a bit. But let's remember what we said on Day 3: Whatever we learn about Jonah always comes back to what it reveals about *us*.

The first part of Jonah's prayer is a prayer of thanksgiving (verses 1-6). It seems odd to thank God for being stuck inside a fish. We might expect Jonah's prayer to be, "I'm sorry, God! Please get me out of this fish!" But, as we explored a couple of days ago, Jonah saw the fish as grace. He had been thrown into the sea. Waves crashed all around, driving him deeper into darkness. It was all over, but then God "snatched

[Jonah] from the jaws of death" (v. 6, NLT). We will look at this aspect of Jonah's prayer tomorrow.

Jonah also appears to pray two separate prayers. As he prays inside the fish, he recounts a prayer he prayed as he was sinking, right before he was gulped up:

You threw me into the ocean depths,
and I sank down to the heart of the sea.
The mighty waters engulfed me;
I was buried beneath your wild and stormy waves.
Then I said, 'O LORD, you have driven me from your presence.
Yet I will look once more toward your holy Temple.' (Jonah 2:3-4, NLT, emphasis mine)

Even though Jonah was engulfed in the waters, he had confidence that God would save him.

Beginning with verse 7, Jonah moves from thanking God to committing to do what God has asked. He will "fulfill all his vows" (v. 9, NLT). Or, as The Message translation puts it, "I'll do what I promised I'd do!" Jonah is telling God he will stop running and go to Nineveh. But is it too late? We'll have to wait to find out. *(Spoiler alert: It's not too late, and good news like that can't wait!)*

We can learn a lot from Jonah's fish prayer. Jonah is sincerely thankful for God's saving grace while he was headed for death. And out of that thankfulness, Jonah is ready to obey God. But one thing is missing: Jonah never says "I'm sorry" for running. Part of him still thinks he is justified in avoiding Nineveh. And while he's thankful to receive God's grace for himself, he's not ready to extend it to others. We will see these feelings bubble up again at the end of the story. As John Goldingay wonders:

Does [Jonah's] failure to say "Sorry, sorry, sorry" suggest that he still has a lot to learn?[14]

Yes, Jonah has more to learn, but God is willing to save it for another day. For now, Jonah has made enough progress in the fish to take the next step forward. God celebrates the small victories in us, even when we think they're not enough. God will keep working on Jonah as they continue their adventure together.

Just like God keeps working on all of us messy, broken people.

> Questions to Ponder:
>
> Take some time to read Jonah's prayer in Jonah 2:1-9. How would you break down what Jonah is saying?
>
> Jonah's prayer includes thankfulness and a commitment to obey God, but lacks repentance. How can you incorporate all three elements in your prayers this week?
>
> What small victory is God celebrating in you? Will you join in the celebration?

---

14 Goldingay.

Day 17:
But God...

**Today's Bible Reading: Jonah 2:1-6
Supporting Passages: Psalm 30; Ephesians 2:1-9**

*But you, O LORD my God,
    snatched me from the jaws of death!*

Many commentators point out that Jonah's prayer echoes words found in the psalms. Since Jonah was familiar with Scripture, he probably had entire psalms memorized. Author Priscilla Shirer says, "In dire circumstances… [Jonah's] mind went straight to God's Word and repeated it out loud."[15]

Jonah's situation also seems to bring some of the psalms to life. For example, Psalm 69:1-2 gives the image of sinking into a sea:

*Save me, O God,
for the floodwaters are up to my neck.
Deeper and deeper I sink into the mire;
I can't find a foothold.
I am in deep water,
and the floods overwhelm me.* (NLT)

Jonah describes this experience when he cries out, "I sank beneath the waves, and the waters closed over me. Seaweed wrapped itself around my head" (Jonah 2:5, NLT). *(By the way, I'd be totally grossed out to have seaweed wrapped around my head!)*

---

15 Shirer, Priscilla. *Jonah: Navigating a Life Interrupted.* Lifeway Press, 2010.

We see another parallel in Psalm 30 when King David writes:

You brought me up from the grave, O LORD.
You kept me from falling into the pit of death. (v. 3, NLT)

David is thanking God for rescuing him from *Sheol*, which is a Hebrew word translated as "the grave" or "death." Jonah thanks God for the same thing when he says, "I called to you from the **land of the dead [Sheol]**, and LORD, you heard me!" (Jonah 2:2, NLT, emphasis mine)

In the first five verses of his prayer, Jonah acknowledges that he was in over his head, both literally and metaphorically. There was no way he could save himself. And then in verse 6, Jonah utters the two most hopeful words in his prayer:

But *you, O LORD my* **God***,*
snatched me from the jaws of death! (NLT, emphasis mine)

But God…

Aren't those two words beautiful? They bring hope to hopeless situations.

The Israelites were enslaved in Egypt for hundreds of years. *But God* rescued them.

In Persia, King Xerxes signed an evil decree to kill all the Jews. *But God* made Esther, a Jewish girl, queen.

And then there is the ultimate "But God…" moment. All the world was broken and messed up by sin. We were hopeless and destined for death—a death we deserved. *But God* stepped into the mess of this world:

By our very nature we were subject to God's anger, just like everyone else. **But God** *is so rich in mercy, and he loved us so much, that even though we were dead because of our sins, he gave us life when he raised Christ from the dead. (It is only*

DAY 17: BUT GOD...

by God's grace that you have been saved!) ... God saved you by his grace when you believed. And you can't take credit for this; it is a gift from God. (Ephesians 2:3–5, 8, NLT)

"But God" are the two greatest words we can hear, but only if we're willing to admit we are helpless to save ourselves.

Jonah has some pride issues. He ran from God because he thought he knew who should get God's grace and who shouldn't. But as he sinks to the bottom of the sea, with seaweed wrapped around his head and waves crashing over him, he realizes he's helpless. He admits he is broken and unable to save himself. And that's when Jonah experiences a "But God" moment.

Recognizing our brokenness is good news. Realizing we have nothing left to give is the best place to be. It's the place where God can step into our mess and begin working on us. That doesn't mean everything will turn out the way we want it to. (Jonah's story didn't end as he expected.) But inviting God into our troubles is so much better than trying to deal with them on our own.

> ### 💬 Questions to Ponder:
>
> How does Jonah admit his helplessness to God in Jonah 2:1-6?
>
> Has God ever worked in an area of your life after you gave up control of it?
>
> Is there an area of life where you need to admit your inability to save yourself? If so, take some time to invite God into that place.

Day 18:
Never Too Late to Return Home (Part I)

Today's Bible Reading: Jonah 2:7-9
Supporting Passage: Luke 15:16-24

As my life was slipping away,
   I remembered the LORD.

Throughout this book, we've been comparing Jonah to the younger brother in Jesus' parable of the prodigal son. (In the second half of the story, Jonah becomes more like the older brother, and we'll also explore that dynamic.) Both Jonah and the younger brother ran from their father. And they both realized their error after hitting rock (or ocean) bottom. For the younger brother, this revelation came while in a pigsty:

The young man became so hungry that even the pods he was feeding the pigs looked good to him. But no one gave him anything. When he finally came to his senses, he said to himself, "At home even the hired servants have food enough to spare, and here I am dying of hunger! I will go home to my father and say, 'Father, I have sinned against both heaven and you, and I am no longer worthy of being called your son. Please take me on as a hired servant.'" (Luke 15:16-19, NLT)

As the younger brother is about to take in a mouthful of pig slop, he remembers how good he had it at his father's house. So he decides to head back home. But he's not delusional. He knows how bad he messed up, and he doesn't expect to be greeted with forgiveness. At best, he hopes his father will hire him to do some work around the farm. But, to his surprise, Dad had a welcome home party waiting for him!

DAY 18: NEVER TOO LATE TO RETURN HOME (PART 1)

While inside the fish, Jonah also remembered all the ways God came through for him:

As my life was slipping away,
  I remembered the LORD.
And my earnest prayer went out to you
    in your holy Temple. (Jonah 2:7, NLT, emphasis mine)

In the Bible, the act of remembering is not passive. There are many instances of God "remembering" a promise he made. But that doesn't mean God is like the absent-minded professor. When God remembers, it means he is ready to *act* on his promise. And when Jonah remembers God, it propels him into action. From inside the belly of a fish, Jonah recommits to following God. He promises to "Offer sacrifices to [God] with songs of praise" (v. 9).

After the fish vomited Jonah out, Jonah may have headed straight to the temple to offer his sacrifice. And back on Day 12, we talked about how the sailors made a sacrifice to God after the storm calmed. Can you imagine if Jonah crossed paths with the sailors while at the temple?

The sailors look at Jonah and say, "Hey! It's the guy who caused the storm! Man, sorry again for throwing you overboard... But look! We're worshiping the LORD now! By the way, how'd you make it out of that alive?!"

"It's a long story, guys," replies Jonah. "But right now, I need to offer this sacrifice and get to Nineveh ASAP!"

(Yes, this is a bit of Jonah fan fiction. But it's fun to imagine!)

Sometimes we feel like we've messed up too much to return to God. The truth is, we are all one choice away from a mouthful of pig slop. (Or, in Jonah's case, seawater!) I've had moments where I woke up in a proverbial pigsty and wondered, "How did I get here? How can God ever love me after everything I just did?" But even a pigsty can be a place of grace if it helps us come to our senses and remember God. The same goes for the belly of a fish. In the song "Dare You to Move," Switchfoot captures the beauty of finding grace in the mess:

Maybe redemption has stories to tell
Maybe forgiveness is right where you fell
Where can you run to escape from yourself?
Where you gonna go? Where you gonna go?
Salvation is here[16]

If you feel far from God right now, take some time to remember him as Jonah did. Remember all the ways he's been good to you. All the ways he's shown you grace throughout your story, even in the hard parts (maybe especially in the hard parts). Then brush yourself off and head back home. God has a party waiting for all the Jonahs and younger brothers.

It's never too late for messy people to return home because God doesn't want anyone left out.

 Questions to Ponder:

When the younger brother "came to his senses," what do you think he realized? When Jonah "remembered the LORD," what do you think he remembered?

Have you ever thought you messed up too badly for God to love you? In those times, how can remembering God help you to return to him and accept his grace?

---

16 Switchfoot. "Dare You to Move." *The Beautiful Letdown*, Charlie Peacock, John Fields.

Day 19:
Self-Righteous Prayer (Or, Did Jonah Just Diss the Ninevites?)

Today's Bible Reading: Jonah 2:8-9
Supporting Passage: Luke 18:9-14

Those who worship false gods
  turn their backs on all God's mercies.

This week we've been looking at Jonah's prayer from inside the belly of the fish. We've seen several good things come about from Jonah's conversation with God. Jonah thanks God for rescuing him and promises to do what God has asked him to do (namely, go to Nineveh).

On the flip side, there are some negative elements to Jonah's prayer that we can also learn from. Jonah never says he's sorry for jumping on a boat and heading in the opposite direction of Nineveh. While he feels the gravity of disobeying God, he still doesn't agree with the job God has for him. And Jonah doubles down on this attitude when he insults the Ninevites toward the end of his prayer.

This backhanded dig is hard to catch at first because it's disguised as "religious talk." (A great reminder that even our prayers can be laced with passive-aggressiveness.) Before we take a look at it, I want to be upfront and say that not all commentators share this view. I admit I could be wrong about Jonah's motives. Let's explore it together, and then you can let me know what *you* think!

Here is the verse in question:

*"Those who worship false gods
turn their backs on all God's mercies.
But I will offer sacrifices to you with songs of praise,
and I will fulfill all my vows.
For my salvation comes from the LORD alone."* (Jonah 2:8-9, NLT)

Those words seem innocent enough, but they have a tinge of self-righteousness to them. As we saw from Jonah's encounter with the sailors, there were an array of deities in the ancient world. The Ninevites had their own set of gods they worshiped. Jonah was essentially saying, *"Those Ninevites* turned their backs on you, God. They don't deserve your grace. But me? Well, *I* will do the right thing and offer sacrifices to you." Jonah was reminding God that going to Nineveh still wasn't such a good idea! Tim Keller puts it like this:

[Jonah] sees the literal idols that the pagans worship and doesn't see the more subtle idols in his own life that keep him from fully grasping that he too, just like the heathen, lives only, equally by God's grace.[17]

As I read this part of Jonah's prayer, I can't help but think of Jesus' parable of the Pharisee and tax collector. Like Jonah, the Pharisee puts the focus of his prayer on the brokenness of other people:

*The Pharisee stood by himself and prayed this prayer: "I thank you, God, that I am not like **other people**—cheaters, sinners, adulterers. I'm certainly not like that tax collector! **I** fast twice a week, and **I** give you a tenth of my income."* (Luke 18:11-12, NLT, emphasis mine)

But the despised tax collector kept the focus on his own brokenness. Instead of comparing himself to others, he said, "O God, be merciful to me, for I am a sinner" (Luke 18:13, NLT).

Earlier I mentioned that not all commentators agree on what Jonah's

---

17 Keller, pp. 81-82.

DAY 19: SELF-RIGHTEOUS PRAYER (OR, DID JONAH JUST DISS THE NINEVITES?)

motives are in this part of the prayer. Some think Jonah is being genuine, and maybe he was. But do you know why I believe Jonah's prayer contained a hidden insult to the Ninevites? Because I know how self-righteous *my* prayers can be! So often, my prayer time is spent telling God about all the great stuff I did or how *those people* over there just don't get it. "God, please change them," I pray.

I can't help but smile when I read this part of Jonah's prayer. I smile, not because I'm better than Jonah, but because I *am* Jonah. I realize how often I compare myself to others to prove I'm not such a mess.

I also smile because God hears Jonah's imperfect prayer. God knows Jonah still doesn't get why he's being sent to Nineveh. And yet, God commands the fish to vomit Jonah out. That gives me hope.

It means God doesn't give up on broken, messy, self-righteous people (like me).

 Questions to Ponder:

What do you think Jonah was saying in Jonah 2:8-9?

In Jesus' parable, what is the difference between the prayer of the Pharisee and the prayer of the tax collector? What can you learn about prayer from this story?

Take some time today to remember that God hears every imperfect prayer. No matter where you find yourself, he won't give up on you.

Day 20:
Don't Go Diving for Buried Sins

Today's Bible Reading: Jonah 2:6; 2:10
Supporting Passage: Micah 7:14-20

Then the LORD ordered the fish to spit Jonah out onto the beach.

My wife, Diana, thinks the ocean is fascinating. I find it nightmarish.

We once watched a show on Netflix that explored the creatures living in the deepest depths of the ocean. I had to look away a few times. *(Not even kidding.)*

Did you know there's a parasite down there that enters a fish through its gills and proceeds to eat the fish's tongue? Oh, it gets worse. The parasite then grows and *becomes* the fish's tongue. So when the fish opens its mouth, you see a tongue that's alive! (I promise I'm not making this up. It's called a Cymothoa exigua. I'll spare you a picture, but Google it if you're feeling brave.)

I wonder if Jonah came across this little guy as he descended into the sea. Jonah sank so far down that he felt as if he'd reached the ocean floor.

"I sank down to the very roots of the mountains.
I was imprisoned in the earth,
whose gates lock shut forever." (Jonah 2:6, NLT)

Imprisoned by this watery grave, a fish provided by God became Jonah's only haven. (Hopefully that fish didn't have a parasitic tongue, or else Jonah would be in big trouble!) From these depths, Jonah sent up a messy, imperfect prayer to God. And after he prays it, something amazing happens:

And the LORD commanded the fish, and it vomited Jonah onto dry land. (2:10, NIV)

Isn't that verse triumphant? It gives me chills! We don't know how much time passed between Jonah's prayer and God's catch-and-release order. But imagine that moment. Jonah hears a rumbling from inside the fish as the stomach walls start shaking. Then, in an instant, he is launched from the fish like a cannon! Sunlight overtakes the darkness, and Jonah opens his eyes to find himself on a beach. *"Am I alive?"* he thinks, spitting out a mouthful of sand.

Jonah has survived his journey 20,000 leagues under the sea. And now, back on land, he feels a little lighter. Jonah left something down on the ocean floor. What was it? *His sin!* And God wants us to leave our sin down there, too.

In the book of Micah (another Old Testament prophet), God warns Israel of a coming punishment. The leaders have taken advantage of the poor. They have not acted justly, shown mercy, or walked humbly with God. (Micah 6:8)

When the people realize what they've done, they cry out to God in despair. And God listens. He throws their sin to the bottom of the ocean floor:

You will again have compassion on us;
you will tread our sins underfoot
and hurl all our iniquities into the depths of the sea. (Micah 7:19, NIV)

I love how succinctly The Message Version puts it:

You'll sink our sins to the bottom of the ocean.

Sin has a way of haunting us. Old memories enter our minds without warning, filling us with shame and regret. We know God forgives us, but we're still tempted to put on our scuba gear and go diving for buried sins. But God put our sins in a place where we can't get to them. The weight of the water is too crushing at the bottom of the ocean.

Of course, this doesn't mean Jonah emerged from the ocean as a sinless person. (We only have to read the rest of the story to see that isn't the case!) We will never be completely rid of our sin until the beautiful day when God brings his kingdom to earth. But when God's forgiveness washes over us, we are free from being defined by our past.

Jonah ran from God and found himself in the deepest parts of the sea. But God brought him out of the depths, back into the warm sunlight, and forgave him. God gave Jonah a fresh start. He was free to continue the adventure without the weight of his past mistakes dragging him down.

The next time you feel haunted by the memories of old sins, remember where they are. They're swimming with the fish that has a tongue that's alive. As Audio Adrenaline says in their song "Ocean Floor":

They're all behind you
They'll never find you
They're on the ocean floor
Your sins are forgotten
They're on the bottom
Of the ocean floor[18]

Let's leave them down there.

---

18 Audio Adrenaline. "Ocean Floor." *Lift*.

DAY 20: DON'T GO DIVING FOR BURIED SINS

💬 Questions to Ponder:

After Jonah landed back on the beach, what thoughts and emotions do you think he was experiencing?

Are you ever haunted by old sins even though you know you are forgiven? How can you leave those sins at the bottom of the ocean where God put them?

Take a moment to reread Jonah 1:17-2:10. What is one thing you've learned from this section of the story?

Day 21:
The God of Fresh Starts (The Adventure Continues...)

Today's Bible Reading: Jonah 3:1-3

Then the LORD spoke to Jonah a second time: "Get up and go to the great city of Nineveh, and deliver the message I have given you."

Several years ago, I co-wrote a musical for my church based on the book of Jonah called *Jonah & the Wave Breakers*. (You can listen to the cast recording on Spotify!) The first act ended with Jonah being spit up by the fish. During intermission, a friend came up to me and said, "This is great, but I don't know what you're going to do in Act II. Isn't the story pretty much over?"

In pop culture, the story of Jonah usually ends with chapter 2. The events in chapters 3 and 4 may get a brief mention but often get overlooked entirely. Why? It goes back to our fascination with the big fish. Once the fish swims out of the story, we think it's over. But chapter 3 is where things get interesting. So buckle up; we're about to head into dreaded Nineveh with Jonah. Let the curtain rise on Act II!

As Jonah brushes off the sand and unclogs water from his ears, God speaks to him a second time. The first two verses of chapter 3 echo the opening verses of chapter 1. God tells Jonah to go to Nineveh and deliver a message. And once again, the author uses the personal name of God, the LORD (YHWH in Hebrew).

This detail beautifully captures the care God has for us even when

DAY 21: THE GOD OF FRESH STARTS (THE ADVENTURE CONTINUES...)

we run from him. God is still personally involved in Jonah's life. God hasn't left Jonah or given up on him.

Notice how quick God is to put Jonah's past behind him. God doesn't throw Jonah's mistakes back in his face. He doesn't say, "Wow, Jonah, you've really made things difficult for us now. We're three days behind schedule. When this is over and we get back to Israel, you're grounded for life!" No, God doesn't hold grudges. Instead, he gives Jonah another chance to do what's right. And this time, Jonah takes it.

While God pursued Jonah, he didn't forget about the violent atrocities the Ninevites were committing hundreds of miles away. His heart was still breaking for the pain they were inflicting on others. But God's plan involved the Ninevites *and* Jonah. He didn't cancel his plans, but he wasn't in such a hurry that he continued on without Jonah, either. God cares about major cities and minor prophets.

God cares about us, too. But that can be hard to believe when we feel like we've messed things up. As a child, there were times when I got sent to my room because of something I did. When my parents "set me free," they were ready to drop the matter and move on. But I wasn't. I would rather stay in my room and sulk than step out and embrace my second chance.

I do the same thing with God. Sometimes, I feel like I've let him down, and there's no coming back from my mistakes. Sure, maybe God still loves me, but he's better off grounding me for life. I blew my chance at being a part of the work he's doing.

But God doesn't see it that way. The good news of Jonah's story is that it doesn't end when the fish vomits Jonah onto dry land. It doesn't end with God scolding Jonah for his disobedience. God hits the "refresh" button and is ready to continue with the adventure.

God's eagerness to forgive and move on is highlighted in Lamentations 3:22-23:

The steadfast love of the LORD never ceases;
  his mercies never come to an end;
they are new every morning;
  great is your faithfulness. (ESV)

We may see our time inside the fish as wasted, unredeemable time. We may think we strayed too far to be any use to God. But the moment we cry out to him, we are exactly where we need to be. As we shake off the sand and unclog our ears, we just have to wait for God to tell us what to do next.

God is eager to give us a fresh start.

The question is, *will we be eager to step out and embrace it?*

 Questions to Ponder:

How do you think Jonah felt when God spoke to him at the beginning of chapter 3? Why do you think he obeyed God this time?

Is there any area of your life where you feel like you have strayed too far to get a fresh start from God? Take some time today to talk to God about it. How can you embrace the fresh start God is offering you?

Day 22:
Checking It off the To-Do List

Today's Bible Reading: Jonah 3:3-4

On the day Jonah entered the city, he shouted to the crowds: "Forty days from now Nineveh will be destroyed!"

God could have saved some time by having the fish vomit Jonah directly into the city of Nineveh. But, instead, Jonah probably found himself back in Joppa, the place where he hatched his getaway plan. This is an important detail. When God gives us a fresh start, it's still up to us to decide what to do with it. And, as we saw yesterday, "This time Jonah obeyed the LORD's command and went to Nineveh" (3:3, NLT).

When Jonah arrives in the big city, he takes center stage and delivers his message:

"Forty days from now Nineveh will be destroyed!" (Jonah 3:4, NLT)

In the original Hebrew, Jonah's message is only five words long. Some may look at it and think, *Wow! I wish my pastor preached as succinctly as Jonah!*

All kidding aside, Jonah's one-sentence sermon can leave you scratching your head. Tim Mackie points out the oddity of it:

"[Jonah's sermon has] no mention of what the Ninevites have done wrong or of what they should do to respond... And most noticeable, there's no mention of God."[19]

---

19 BibleProject. "Overview: Jonah."

We know God told Jonah to "deliver the message *I* have given you" (v. 2, emphasis mine). And we also know the Ninevites' violent ways were causing horrific suffering in the lives of others. God didn't want to see this brutality continue. He was ready to do something about it. But was this five-word message the *complete* message God gave to Jonah? Or did Jonah put his own Eeyore-style spin on it?

To answer this, we need to remember what kind of story the book of Jonah is. As I said back on Day 2, I think Jonah's story is both historical *and* satirical. Jonah's message to the Ninevites is full of irony. Yes, it contained the truth of God's impending judgment. But it also left out any promise of God's hope. Jonah was not interested in telling the Ninevites how they could avoid calamity. His message dripped with insincerity.

In the movie *Willy Wonka & the Chocolate Factory*, Wonka gives a tour of his factory to five children. One by one, each child meets a tragic fate because of a selfish decision they make. At one point, Mike Teevee is about to shrink himself with a laser so he can go into TV Land. Wonka warns him, "Stop. Don't. Come back." But from his dry, monotone delivery, it's clear that Wonka has no interest in saving Mike. He wants to weed out the bad eggs and get on with life.

This was Jonah's attitude as he delivered his message to the Ninevites. And when imagined in this context, it's both funny and heartbreaking. Jonah wanted to do the bare minimum to get Nineveh checked off his to-do list.

Before I judge Jonah too harshly, I have to hold the mirror up to myself. When have I tried to get away with the least amount of work required?

Sometimes God will put people in my life who are lonely and desperate for connection. I know God wants me to take time out of my day to talk to them. But five minutes into the conversation, I'm already looking for a way out. I have "more important" things to do.

DAY 22: CHECKING IT OFF THE TO-DO LIST

Or what about community service projects? Ten minutes into one and I'm already bored, tired, and thinking about what's for lunch. I did my time, now get me out of here!

Too often, I'm focused on checking tasks off a list rather than loving the people God has put in front of me.

The most ironic part of Jonah's sermon is that he withheld the one thing God extended to him while inside the fish. T.E. Fretheim calls it "a graceless message delivered by one living in the shadow of an experience of grace."[20]

Being trapped inside a watery tomb wasn't enough to stop God's grace from getting to Jonah. And, as we'll see tomorrow, a dry, insincere sermon won't be enough to stop God's grace from getting to the Ninevites.

Because God doesn't want anyone left out.

 Questions to Ponder:

What is your opinion of Jonah's message to the Ninevites? Do you think there were things he purposely left out?

When are you most likely to view something God has asked you to do as an item to be checked off a list? How can you change your perspective and view it as an opportunity to share God's love with others?

---

20   T.E. Fretheim, *The Message of Jonah* (Minneapolis: Augsburg, 1977), 108.

Day 23:
Is This Some Kind of Joke?!

Today's Bible Reading: Jonah 3:4-6

The Ninevites believed God. A fast was proclaimed, and all of them, from the greatest to the least, put on sackcloth.

Yesterday, we saw that Jonah obeyed God and went to Nineveh. But when he got there, he gave a five-word sermon to the Ninevites void of any compassion.

One fascinating thing I discovered in my research is that it would have taken Jonah about a month to travel to Nineveh.[21] As the days passed, maybe Jonah started thinking less about how God saved him and more about how evil the Ninevites were. When he arrived in Nineveh, his fish adventure seemed like a distant memory. It's so easy for self-righteousness to creep back into our lives when we forget all God has done for us.

But Jonah was a success in spite of himself. In another touch of irony, the Ninevites accept Jonah's message and believe God. I imagine Jonah's jaw dropping like a cartoon character's as he thought, *Wait, seriously? Is this some kind of joke?!*

In a sense, the Ninevites' transformation *was* a joke—the kind of wonderful joke that lifts your spirits and makes you laugh with joy. It flips everything upside down. A sulky prophet delivers a threatening message to a terrorist group. We'd expect the Ninevites to take one

---

21 Smith, p. 256.

DAY 23: IS THIS SOME KIND OF JOKE?!

look at Jonah and toss him into their latest torture device. Instead, they begin to mourn their sin. In an instant, hope appears where there was darkness. We can't help but crack a smile at the beauty of God's grace.

There is some backstory that adds to the wonder of this event. Around the time of Jonah's visit, the nation of Assyria fell on hard times. They were at war with other nations and battling political upheaval at home. They were also facing plagues and famine. To the outside world, the Ninevites were a powerhouse. But inside, they were a mess. And the mess is where God does his best work.

God was working on the Ninevites long before he called Jonah to go there. Jonah thought he was walking into a losing battle, but God had secretly stacked the deck in his favor! God knew that *this* moment was the perfect time to show the Ninevites a better way to live. Success didn't rely on Jonah's ability to do everything perfectly. It relied on God. When the angel Gabriel told Mary she would give birth to Jesus, he added, "For nothing will be impossible with God" (Luke 1:37, ESV).

The Ninevites' transformation brings a smile to my face because it means nobody is beyond God's reach. Nobody has to be left out.

Sometimes it doesn't feel that way, does it? There are people—people we love and care about—who want nothing to do with God. It seems impossible that they would ever welcome Jesus into their lives. But we can't see all the ways God is working in their hearts. They look confident and put together on the outside. But on the inside, they may be desperate for hope. Our job is to (imperfectly) share God's compassion with them and leave the outcome up to him.

Jonah had something in common with his enemies. He turned to God when he found himself trapped inside a fish. Jonah didn't know it, but the Ninevites were also experiencing an "inside-a-fish" moment. They were in a unique position to hear a message about God.

Jonah's adventure reminds us that God's grace works best in the mess. In the brokenness. In the lowest of low points.

Now that's something to crack a smile about!

 Questions to Ponder:

What are some ways self-righteousness can creep into your life? How can you stay focused on your need for God's grace rather than the sins of others?

Why do you think the Ninevites accepted Jonah's message so quickly?

Is there anyone in your life who you wish knew God? Today, take some time to pray for them. Remember that God may be working in their hearts in ways you can't see. What are some ways you can show them God's compassion?

Day 24:
God Meets Us Where We're At

Today's Bible Reading: Jonah 3:5-9
Supporting Passage: James 2:14-26

When Jonah's warning reached the king of Nineveh, he rose from his throne, took off his royal robes, covered himself with sackcloth and sat down in the dust.

After Jonah issued his warning in Nineveh, the Ninevites "believed God" (3:5, NIV). Notice it doesn't say they "believed *in* God." The omission of the little word "in" is important. Believing in God is great, but we also need to believe what God tells us and engage in the work he has called us to do.

One Bible verse that has always fascinated me is James 2:19:

You believe that there is one God. Good! Even the demons believe that—and shudder. (NIV)

In this passage, James (the brother of Jesus) talks about how our faith and actions are intertwined. Faith was not meant to be a simple mental exercise where we check all the correct "theological boxes."

When a tragedy strikes, it's typical to see sentiments like "sending prayers" pop up on social media (complete with prayer hand emojis). Non-believers may grow tired of this phrase and see it as an empty platitude or an excuse not to take action. And you know what? In some cases, that's a valid criticism. But it shouldn't be that way because prayer and action are not mutually exclusive.

In the Bible, prayer and action are always connected. People pray and then act according to who they *believe* God to be. This is what the Ninevites did. They didn't do it perfectly, but God honored what they offered him.

Throughout the book of Jonah, God has been referred to as YHWH ("the LORD"). But now, when the Ninevites begin interacting with God, his Hebrew name changes to *Elohim*. Elohim is still a name for Israel's God, but it's less personal. This subtle shift highlights that the Ninevites don't even know the name of Jonah's God yet. But they *do* believe he's not happy with their violent ways. And so, despite not knowing everything about God, they begin taking steps toward him.

The king of Nineveh tells his people to put on sackcloth, go without food or water, and give up their violence. He also encourages everyone to "call urgently on God" (3:8, NIV). The best way to get to know God is to start talking to him!

Some of these practices would have been strange to the Ninevites. Like the sailors in chapter 1, the Assyrian nation had their own gods and religious customs. Fasting was not something they did, but maybe they knew it was a Hebrew practice and decided to give it a try.[22]

How did the Ninevites know a second chance was possible? They may have questioned Jonah to see if there was any hope of forgiveness. (I imagine Jonah responding begrudgingly with, "Oh, I *suppose*...") But there was still no guarantee of a happy ending.

It didn't matter. The Ninevites acted anyway. I love the insightful words of the king of Nineveh:

Who knows? *God **may** yet relent and with compassion turn from his fierce anger so that we will not perish.* (3:9, NIV, emphasis mine)

His words echo those of the ship captain who wakes Jonah from his

---
22 Smith, p. 263.

sleep and says, "Get up and call on your god! Maybe he will take notice of us so that we will not perish" (1:6, NIV).

Once again, it's the non-believers in this story who believe God, take action, and have hope that he will respond with compassion. And that's exactly what God does! The Ninevites may not have understood every action they were taking. (And, as we'll see tomorrow, they took some things to ridiculous extremes.) But God could see their hearts.

When we take action, we won't always get it right. Every person in the Bible who took a step of faith got tripped up at some point. But God continued to work with them. He doesn't want perfection because he knows that's impossible. He just wants us to keep following him.

God will take our imperfect actions and meet us where we're at.

> ### Questions to Ponder:
>
> What do you think is the difference between believing *in* God and *believing* God? What are the two examples in James 2:14-26 of people whose faith and actions worked together?
>
> Dallas Willard has said, "Grace is not opposed to effort, it is opposed to earning."[23] How do you think that idea applies to stepping out and taking action?
>
> Is there any action you believe God wants you to take, but you are afraid you'll mess it up? How can you take a step, knowing God will meet you where you're at?

---

23 Willard, Dallas. *The Great Omission: Reclaiming Jesus's Essential Teachings on Discipleship.* HarperOne, 2014.

Day 25:
The Devotional About Animals

Today's Bible Reading: Jonah 3:7-9

Do not let people or animals, herds or flocks, taste anything; do not let them eat or drink. But let people and animals be covered with sackcloth.

A few days ago, I shared that my wife, Diana, loves the ocean, while I find it creepy. She also loves animals and can tell you random facts about them. The closest I get to wildlife is watching nature shows from the comfort of my couch. And even that scares me. (Clearly, Diana is the more adventurous of the two of us.)

The book of Jonah is filled with lots of over-the-top moments. The author uses these extreme situations to show a contrast between Jonah and the people he interacts with. One moment that makes me raise an eyebrow is when the king of Nineveh declares a fast... *and orders all of the animals in the city to join in.* This detail is easy to brush past, but I want to slow down and explore it. So I dedicate today's devotional to all you animal lovers out there!

The king includes animals in two of his instructions to Nineveh: fasting and wearing sackcloth. Dressing in sackcloth (rough material made of goat's hair) was a way to express sorrow. In ancient times, animals sometimes wore sackcloth to join in a nation's mourning.

Fasting was a different story. As we saw yesterday, fasting was not a common practice in the Assyrian culture. But the Ninevites knew it was something the Jewish people did. As one of the palace officials is drawing up the decree, I imagine him asking the king, "And what about the animals?"

"What about them?" the king replies.

"Well... should they do the fast thing too?"

The king thinks for a moment, then shrugs. "Yes, let's do everything we can. Who knows? God may yet relent and with compassion turn from his fierce anger so that we will not perish."

"Oh, that's good," says the official. "I'm going to put that line in there too."

The Ninevites were desperate. They may have assumed fasting was a way of appeasing God. If the animals joined in, maybe their chances of a positive outcome would increase. While fasting is never about manipulating God, it wouldn't be a stretch for the Ninevites to go down that line of thinking. If only they had someone to help them through this...

Oh wait, they did! Where's Jonah?

Part of a prophet's job is to guide people back to God. When Jonah saw how eager the Ninevites were to turn to God, he should have sprung into action. He should have told them more about who YHWH was. He should have smiled when the Ninevites made their animals fast and said, "Wow, I love your commitment! But let me teach you the heart behind this..." Instead, Jonah is silent, leaving the Ninevites to throw spaghetti at the wall to see what sticks.

Maybe Jonah was left speechless by the Ninevites' quick turn. Or maybe he was secretly hoping they would mess this part up, and it would be too little, too late. But God always accepts a broken and contrite heart. (Psalm 51:17)

Jonah didn't actively hurt the Ninevites, but he didn't try to help them either. And as with everything in this story, Jonah's foibles reflect back on us. When do we use silence to set people up to fail?

Imagine a co-worker is up for the same promotion that I am. If I catch an error on one of her reports, do I let her know? Or do I laugh to myself and leave it for the boss to find?

What if I see a friend going down a path of destruction? It might be easier to keep quiet and let him deal with the consequences of his choices. But shouldn't I try to warn him of what's ahead in a gentle, loving way?

When God handed down his Law to the Israelites, he reminded them to get involved when people needed help. Here is one example he gives (and it includes a reference to animals, our theme for today!):

If you see that your neighbor's donkey or ox has collapsed on the road, **do not look the other way***. Go and help your neighbor get it back on its feet!* (Deuteronomy 22:4, NLT, emphasis mine)

It's easy to stay silent out of spite, fear, or convenience. But as Jesus followers, the standard isn't simply to *not* hurt others. It's to love them sacrificially as he did, even when it costs us.

I guess Diana is right: Animals *are* interesting!

DAY 25: THE DEVOTIONAL ABOUT ANIMALS

 Questions to Ponder:

Why do you think the king of Nineveh included the animals in the fast?

Can you think of a situation in your life where someone spoke up to offer you guidance? What did it cost them?

Is your silence setting up anyone to fail? What might it cost you to speak up?

Bonus Question: What's your favorite animal? (Just wanted to break the tension after that last question!)

Day 26:
The God-Sized City in the Good Potter's Hands

Today's Bible Reading: Jonah 3:10
Supporting Passage: Jeremiah 18:1-10

When God saw what [the Ninevites] had done and how they had put a stop to their evil ways, he changed his mind and did not carry out the destruction he had threatened.

Over the past few days, we've been looking at the Ninevites' amazing transformation. They accepted Jonah's message and took steps toward changing their violent behavior. When God saw this, he decided to spare Nineveh from destruction. As we'll see when we get to chapter 4, Jonah is not happy about this "change of plans." But God's desire for Nineveh was always that they would accept his peace offering.

When God called Jonah to go to Nineveh, he referred to it as a "great city" (1:2; 3:2, NIV). The word "great" can mean "big" or "significant," and Nineveh was both of those things. But it has another meaning as well. In Hebrew, the phrase means "a city great to God." L.C. Allen calls the city of Nineveh "God-sized,"[24] and I think that's a beautiful way of putting it.

God loved the city of Nineveh. He created and loved each individual Ninevite, just as he created and loves you. But if that's true, then the parts of the Bible that talk about God judging people seem harsh.

---
24   L.C. Allen, *Joel, Obadiah, Jonah, and Micah* (Grand Rapids: Eerdmans, 1976), 221.

DAY 26: THE GOD-SIZED CITY IN THE GOOD POTTER'S HANDS

We struggle to make sense of a God who loves completely yet renders judgment. I confess this is an issue I wrestle with all the time! But whenever there's a tension in the Bible, I try to embrace it and look deeper.

In his sermon series on Jonah, Tim Mackie says that although judgment and love seem like opposites, they are not.[25] The true opposite of judgment, he argues, is apathy. When God saw the Ninevites brutalizing other people—people created in his image—the most loving thing he could do was judge their behavior. An apathetic shoulder shrug from God wouldn't be love.

The brutality of the Ninevites wasn't just directed at other nations. They were the victims as well. There was violence *within* Nineveh.[26] The powerful preyed on the weak. No group is immune from destroying each other from the inside. When the Apostle Paul wrote to the Christians in Galatia, he issued this warning:

If you bite and devour each other, watch out or you will be destroyed by each other. (Galatians 5:15, NIV)

We destroy each other with words, and we destroy each other with actions. But the lesson we learn from Nineveh is there's always hope to change. Jonah knew this. It's why he didn't want to warn Nineveh about the coming judgment. If God was giving Nineveh a 40-day window, it meant there was still hope for a happy ending, and Jonah didn't like that. He refused to see Nineveh as God-sized. Is there any person (or group) we refuse to see as God-sized?

A couple of centuries after Jonah's adventure, God spoke through the prophet Jeremiah. God compared himself to a potter, and we are the clay in his hands. That can be a scary image until we remember his compassion. Maybe God thought back to Nineveh when he spoke these words:

---

25 *Thrones and Ashes - Amazing Jonah*, Tim Mackie, 17 Aug. 2017, https://youtu.be/7AgpZwzPyPI.

26 Keller, p. 89.

If I announce that a certain nation or kingdom is to be uprooted, torn down, and destroyed, **but then that nation renounces its evil ways, I will not destroy it as I had planned.** (Jeremiah 18:7-8, NLT, emphasis mine)

We are God-sized people in the hands of a good potter. God created each one of us with dignity. He knows us, and he loves us. And it breaks his heart when we do things to hurt and destroy each other.

But Jonah's story reminds us of the good news. There's hope when we recognize our brokenness and allow the potter to shape us. When we bring our mess to God, he cleans us up. He exchanges our clothes—dripping with stinky pig slop—for a fresh robe. And he throws us a party like we've never seen.

If God can do it for Nineveh, he can do it for us.

He truly doesn't desire for anyone to be left out.

 Questions to Ponder:

Have you ever thought of yourself as a "person great to God" or a "God-sized person"? Would anything change if you viewed yourself this way? Would anything change if you viewed *other people* this way?

What are some ways humans "bite and devour each other"? Why do you think this breaks God's heart?

Are you dealing with any mess today? If so, take some time to bring it to God and remember he is the good potter.

Day 27:
Jonah Got What He Wanted!

Today's Bible Reading: Jonah 3:4; 3:10

Jonah began by going a day's journey into the city, proclaiming, "Forty more days and Nineveh will be overthrown." ... When God saw what they did and how they turned from their evil ways, he relented and did not bring on them the destruction he had threatened.

It may surprise some people to learn that the Bible is filled with humorous wordplay. Words are intentionally chosen to drive home a point in a clever way. Unfortunately, much of this goes over a modern reader's head if they don't know Hebrew or Greek. (And this is coming from someone who knows zero Hebrew or Greek, so no judgment. Commentaries are my cheat codes!)

An example of this wit is found in the one-sentence sermon Jonah delivers to the Ninevites:

"Forty more days and Nineveh will be overthrown." (Jonah 3:4, NIV)

The message seems straightforward enough. But the Hebrew word for "overthrown" (also translated as "overturned" in some versions) has more than one meaning. It can mean "destroyed," and that's the meaning we naturally assign to it when we read Jonah's speech. But it can also mean "transformed" or "changed." Biblical scholar Douglas Stuart says Jonah's words could carry the idea that "in forty more days Nineveh would *have a change of heart.*"[27]

---

27 D. Stuart. *Hosea-Jonah,* WBC (Dallas: Word, 1987), 489.

I know I keep saying this, but it's so important to remember: The author of Jonah is using humor to get his message across. We are supposed to smile at wonderful ironies like this. Jonah tells the Ninevites they will be overturned. And that is exactly what happens. They *turn* from their violence, and God showers them with compassion. Jonah was right… just not in the way he hoped he would be!

Poor Jonah. *He can't catch a break!* Every time he does something to sabotage the Ninevites, he gets pounded by another wave of God's grace.

At the end of the book of Jonah, God describes the Ninevites as people who "cannot tell their right hand from their left" (4:11, NIV). This doesn't mean they were innocent or oblivious to the atrocities they were committing. But it did mean they were lost and needed to be found by God.

The Ninevites remind me of the wild, awful kids in the book *The Best Christmas Pageant Ever*. The story centers around the Herdmans—six siblings who behave terribly. One day, they go to church (to raid the free snacks) and end up volunteering to be in the annual Christmas pageant. At first the parents of the other children are horrified and complain to the pastor. How can these "bad kids" be allowed to participate in such a holy event?

But as time goes on, the church members begin to see the Christmas story through the eyes of the Herdman kids. They are reminded that Christmas is about Jesus coming into this world to rescue messy, broken people. People like the Herdmans who show up to Sunday school just to get free snacks. But also people like the good churchgoers who try to leave the bad kids out. In the end, the town decides it was the best Christmas pageant ever. They had a front seat to God's grace, and it filled them with joy.

Jonah had a front seat to God's grace as well. The wild, awful Ninevites were found by God, but Jonah missed it. His view of grace was obstructed by his hatred of the Ninevites. How can God have compassion for these "bad people"?

Jonah wanted the Ninevites destroyed. God wanted them transformed.

Which one do we want for our enemies?

 Questions to Ponder:

What do you think of the multiple meanings of the word "overthrown"? Which one do you think Jonah had in mind?

Have you ever had a front row seat to someone being transformed by God's grace? How did it affect you?

We may not hope for our enemies to be physically "destroyed" as Jonah did. But in what other ways do we hope for the worst for those we disagree with?

Day 28:
But Did It Really Matter?

Today's Bible Reading: 2 Kings 18:13-2 Kings 19

In the fourteenth year of King Hezekiah's reign, King Sennacherib of Assyria came to attack the fortified towns of Judah and conquered them.

Before moving on to the fourth and final chapter of Jonah, I want to spend today exploring a question: *What happened to the Ninevites?*

We know the Ninevites made an amazing transformation. They put an end to their violent ways and turned to God. But did this change of heart last? And what does the answer to that question have to do with us?

About forty years after Jonah's visit to Nineveh, the Assyrian nation invaded Israel.[28] Israel's king, Menahem, managed to keep them at bay by bribing the Assyrian king with money (2 Kings 15:19–20). A few years later, Sennacherib—another Assyrian king—threatened Jerusalem and mocked God in the process. (The story of how God intervened and saved Jerusalem is the topic of today's Bible reading.) Sadly, Assyria eventually did manage to conquer the northern kingdom and drag the Israelites into captivity.

We can imagine Jonah shaking his head at this and saying, "I told you so, God! Should've listened to me!"

The Ninevites' change was short-lived. They went back to their old,

---

28 Smith, p. 262.

DAY 28: BUT DID IT REALLY MATTER?

violent ways. So did Jonah's trip to Nineveh matter in the end? Or was it all a waste of time?

Following God is never a waste of time, even when we stumble and fall.

It's easy to be skeptical of a change in other people. When we hear about *that* person turning over a new leaf, we're tempted to take a wait-and-see attitude. *He wrecked his life once, after all. She is just a liar, and that's all there is to it.*

It's great if they changed, we think. *But let's give it a week and see what happens.* And if they do slip up, we question whether their attempt at change was genuine at all.

But before I judge the Ninevites (or anyone else, for that matter), I need to look at my own struggle to follow God.

In the book *A Faith of Her Own: Women of the Old Testament*, J. Ellsworth Kalas talks about the prophet Deborah. (Her story is found in Judges 4–5.) Under her courageous leadership, the Israelites returned to God and had peace in their land for forty years. And then, at the turn of a page, the Israelites stumbled and were back to where they started.

Kalas wonders if Deborah's tenure in Israel was a waste of time. He writes:

So after forty years was Deborah a waste, someone of whom we could say, "all is vanity," nothing but a passing breath? By no means. ... Deborah won the battle in her day. A remarkable woman ... But so it is with all those who love, live, fight, and pray for goodness and justice. ... **And if they win the battle for forty years, thanks be to God! Sometimes it is a grand feat to win for forty minutes, especially in the private battlefield of our own souls.**[29]

---

[29] Kalas, J. Ellsworth. *A Faith of Her Own: Women of the Old Testament.* Abingdon Press, 2012.

I love that last sentence. In my own struggles against sin, forty minutes can feel like an eternity. And in the moments I do succumb to going my way instead of God's, I feel defeated.

Have I made any progress at all? I think. *Shouldn't I be better by now?*

Why do I still let my anger get the best of me when I interact with that person? *I don't love people the way Jesus did.*

Why am I still prone to putting myself ahead of my family? *I'm so selfish.*

The truth is, we *do* make progress, though it's hard to see it in ourselves. But that will never erase our need for God's grace. The more we follow Jesus, the more we recognize how broken we are. And the more we realize how broken we are, the deeper we experience Jesus' love for us.

What happened in Nineveh is something to celebrate. It was genuine, even if it didn't last forever. As we'll see tomorrow, Jonah is about to run from God the same way he did at the start of the story. But that doesn't mean his return to God inside the fish wasn't genuine.

If you feel defeated by your lack of progress, remember that God's love is greater than your sin. He doesn't give up on his children. He knows how frail we are. We are messy, broken people. Our small moments of faithfulness matter more than we know. And when we stumble and fail for the 70,620th time, all we have to do is cry out to God.

Grace isn't linear. It comes in waves.

DAY 28: BUT DID IT REALLY MATTER?

> 💬 **Questions to Ponder:**
>
> What do you think of what happened to the Ninevites in the years after Jonah's visit?
>
> Do you know anyone who is trying to make a positive change in their life? How can you encourage them through the ups and downs of the journey?
>
> Do you feel you should be "better by now" in any area of life? Take some time to tell God about it. Remember, his grace is bigger than your mess.
>
> Take a moment to reread Jonah 3. What is one thing you've learned from this section of the story?

Day 29:
The Reason Why There's a Fourth Chapter of Jonah

Today's Bible Reading: Jonah 4
Supporting Passage: Luke 15:25-32

But to Jonah this seemed very wrong, and he became angry.

Fairy tales are known for their "happily ever after" endings. But Bible stories—even humorous ones like Jonah—don't wrap up so neatly. This is one reason why I take the Bible seriously. It's full of messy stories because real life is messy!

If the story of Jonah concluded with chapter 3, we'd have our happy ending. The Ninevites turn from their evil ways, and God showers them with mercy. *Yay!* Even if Jonah wasn't thrilled, we figure he would take the win and call it a day. But that's not how it ends. The story continues with chapter 4, and Jonah is burning with anger.

Jonah 4 is my favorite chapter of the story. All the characters exit, leaving only two on the stage for the final scene: YHWH and Jonah. Everything in the story has been leading up to this moment. This whole adventure wasn't just about the Ninevites. It was God's rescue mission for Jonah as well.

I said Jonah 4 is my favorite chapter of the story, but that's not giving it enough credit. It's one of my favorite chapters of *the entire Bible*. In Jonah 4, we see the tenderness of God on display. There are plenty of other places in the Bible where we see this tenderness, but Jonah 4

DAY 29: THE REASON WHY THERE'S A FOURTH CHAPTER OF JONAH

always leaves me gaping in amazement. I smile at Jonah's ridiculous stubbornness. And then I weep because I see that same stubbornness in myself.

God's compassion for the Ninevites seemed "very wrong" to Jonah (4:1). Why?

Maybe Jonah thought the Ninevites were pulling the wool over God's eyes. He imagined the Ninevites making funny faces behind God's back, saying, "Nah-nah-nah-nah-nah-naaaaah! You bought our little act!" We hate to see other people get away with something, especially when we try so hard to be good.

Throughout our adventure, I've compared Jonah to the younger brother in Jesus' parable of the prodigal son. Jonah ran from God, and God welcomed him back with open arms. But now we see a shift and Jonah becomes the older brother. When the father welcomes home his son and throws him a party, the older brother refuses to celebrate. For years he has worked hard while his younger brother lived a carefree life. He complains to his father:

> *"All these years I've slaved for you and never once refused to do a single thing you told me to. And in all that time you never gave me even one young goat for a feast with my friends. Yet when this son of yours comes back after squandering your money on prostitutes, you celebrate by killing the fattened calf!"* (Luke 15:29-30, NLT)

The older brother—like Jonah—kept a scorecard of everything he did right. He also kept one of everything other people did wrong. I keep scorecards far too often. I relegate people to the "naughty" list while justifying why I belong on the "nice."

I think part of the problem is that as humans, our love is finite. So we try to one-up each other to earn the approval of others. *If I'm going to win, somebody else has to lose.* It's an easy trap to get caught in.

Maybe the older brother thought his dad wouldn't love him as much now that his little brother was back. But the father obliterates this idea as he pleads with his son to come join the party:

"His father said to him, 'Look, dear son, you have always stayed by me, and **everything I have is yours.** *We had to celebrate this happy day. For your brother was dead and has come back to life! He was lost, but now he is found!'"* (Luke 15:31-32, NLT, emphasis mine)

The story of the prodigal son wasn't over once the younger brother returned home. The older brother was still lost, and his father wasn't about to give up on him.

God wasn't giving up on Jonah either. *That's why there's a Jonah chapter 4!* Once the Ninevites were safely home, God went back out to find Jonah.

God's love is infinite. It's big enough to include the Ninevites *and* Jonah. It's deep enough to include the younger brothers *and* the older brothers.

God's love is big enough for everyone, and that includes you.

Why is there a fourth chapter of Jonah? Because God doesn't want anyone left out.

 Questions to Ponder:

I shared my reasons why I think the story of Jonah continues after chapter 3. What reasons can you think of?

How are Jonah and the older brother similar? Why do you think they were so angry at God's kindness toward others?

In what ways do you see the "older brother" show up in your life?

Day 30:
Naming Our Enemies

Today's Bible Reading: Jonah 4:1-3
Supporting Passage: Matthew 5:38-48

So [Jonah] complained to the LORD about it: "Didn't I say before I left home that you would do this, LORD? That is why I ran away to Tarshish!"

Yesterday, I said I smile at Jonah's ridiculousness but weep when I see his traits inside myself. God shows compassion to the Ninevites, and Jonah responds in anger. He stomps his feet and says, "Ugh! I knew you would do this, God! This is why I ran away in the first place!" I laugh at Jonah's anger because it seems so unreasonable. *Why can't you be happy for the Ninevites, Jonah?!*

I can shake my head at Jonah, but that's because the Ninevites aren't real to me. They are characters in a story. When someone says the name "Ninevites," I don't have an emotional reaction. I haven't seen the devastation they've caused. I haven't experienced the pain they've inflicted on others. So, of course, it's pretty cool when God forgives them.

But what about when I hear a name that *does* affect me emotionally? *Oh, well, that's a different story… My anger is totally justified then!*

When Jesus gave his Sermon on the Mount, he flipped the standard way of doing things upside-down. One of his most famous teachings from that sermon is about loving our enemies:

You have heard the law that says, "Love your neighbor" and hate your enemy. But

I say, love your enemies! Pray for those who persecute you! (Matthew 5:43-44, NLT)

We've become so familiar with those words that they sound cliche. We nod our heads in agreement without giving a thought to who those enemies may be.

The problem is, the concept of "enemies" is elusive. The word seems so harsh. We imagine enemies as faceless soldiers on a battlefield somewhere. *I* don't have enemies... I just have people I can't stand!

Throughout the *Harry Potter* series, the villain Voldemort is referred to as "He-Who-Must-Not-Be-Named." He's so evil the other characters don't want to speak his name. Are there any specific people (or groups) your friends are hesitant to mention in front of you? If their name comes up, it will launch you into a rant about how terrible they are. Maybe it's someone you assume God is not happy with for some reason.

It could be as benign as the guy who cuts you off in traffic or the grocery store cashier who moves at a sloth-like pace. Maybe it's a difficult family member or an annoying neighbor. Or maybe it's a group of people you blame for all the world's troubles. (It's interesting that the Ninevites were a different race *and* religion from Jonah.) If we say we don't have enemies, we are probably defining the word too narrowly.

Jesus' command, as simple as it sounds, challenges us all to consider who our enemies might be. (As I type these words, people in my own life are coming to mind. Don't worry, it's not you!) We can't love our enemies until we name them and admit our feelings to God. When we let God into those messy places in our hearts, he can begin to change us from the inside out. It's impossible to love our enemies without him.

I need to make one more point about loving your enemies. In this broken world, people are put into horrific situations. If someone has abused you, loving your enemies is not about condoning their actions.

DAY 30: NAMING OUR ENEMIES

It's not about returning to an unsafe environment to be abused again. Sometimes, we need to love our enemies from a distance. If you find yourself in this situation, I encourage you not to go through it alone. Find a safe community to help you walk through a process of healing. Forgiveness liberates the forgiver as much as the forgiven.

Naming our enemies allows us to relate to Jonah's anger. And it prepares us to hear God's tender response in this final chapter of the story. Jonah is about to see his enemies through the eyes of God.

The way we love our enemies looks different in each situation. But it always starts with seeing them as a person who matters to God.

 Questions to Ponder:

How do you define the word "enemy"? Who is the "He-Who-Must-Not-Be-Named" person or group for you?

Do you find it hard to understand Jonah's anger and hatred toward the Ninevites? Does it become more relatable when you name your own enemies?

What would it look like for you to love your enemy in your specific situation? If you're not sure yet, it's okay. Continue to reflect on that question as you go through the final days of this devotional.

Day 31:
God Can't Win!

Today's Bible Reading: Jonah 4:1-3
Supporting Passage: Exodus 34:1-10

"I knew that you are a gracious and compassionate God, slow to anger and abounding in love, a God who relents from sending calamity."

Jonah 4 begins with Jonah unleashing an angry prayer at God. Jonah is spiraling downward, but he gets one thing right: He is brutally honest with God. When I feel angry or frustrated, talking to God is the last thing I want to do. But maybe the times I feel like praying the least are the times when I need to pray the most. God was not scared off by Jonah's anger, and he's not scared off by ours, either. God can take whatever we throw at him.

And boy, did Jonah throw a lot at him. During his prayer, Jonah makes a passive-aggressive dig at God. Back on Day 6, we talked about how "the LORD" is God's personal name, which he revealed to Moses on Mount Sinai. God was about to make a covenant with Israel, and he wanted his people to know him intimately:

Then the LORD came down ... and proclaimed his name, the LORD. And he passed in front of Moses, proclaiming, "The LORD, the LORD, the compassionate and gracious God, slow to anger, abounding in love and faithfulness, maintaining love to thousands, and forgiving wickedness, rebellion and sin. Yet he does not leave the guilty unpunished; he punishes the children and their children for the sin of the parents to the third and fourth generation." (Exodus 34:5-7, NIV)

DAY 31: GOD CAN'T WIN!

Through his name, God revealed two primary things about his character: (1) He is compassionate and quick to forgive, and (2) he judges sin. As we've discussed, these two things *seem* like opposites, but they are both attributes of his love. A loving God's heart breaks when people act in evil ways toward each other.

So what is Jonah's dig at God? In his anger, Jonah quotes God's name, but he leaves an important part out. Look at the similarities between what God says about himself and what Jonah says about God:

I knew that you are a **gracious and compassionate** *God,* **slow to anger and abounding in love**… (4:2, NIV, emphasis mine)

Jonah talks about God's compassion and grace. But he *purposely omits* the part about God not leaving "the guilty unpunished."[30] Sometimes we make more of a statement by what we *don't say* than what we say.

Imagine a son making a toast at his father's 80th birthday celebration. The son talks about what a brilliant businessman his father is, but he makes no mention of him being a good dad. After the speech, we might assume there is some unspoken family drama going on.

Jonah's prayer was doing the same thing. It was Jonah's backhanded way of saying to God, "You say you take sin seriously, but you really don't. Justice is not a part of who you are, even though you claim it is."

In today's culture, most people are cool with God's love but recoil when they come across anything about God's judgment. They wonder how a God who judges can be good. And if you struggle with that question, it's okay. I don't want to dismiss it with easy, pat answers. It's a question worth wrestling with. But remarkably, Jonah had no issues with God's judgment. It was God's *forgiveness and compassion* that made Jonah question God's goodness. As author Skye Jethani explains:

Jonah did not run away because the Lord is **wrathful** *but because he is* **merciful**.

---
30   Keller, pp. 105.

He knew that YHWH would be gracious even to the pagan, wicked people of Nineveh whom Jonah felt deserved no compassion and no more chances. Jonah wanted justice and he was angry that God offered his enemies grace. In Jonah's mind, the real problem with God wasn't his anger, but the fact that he wasn't angry enough.[31]

Sometimes we don't like the idea of a judging God. But there are other times when, like Jonah, we don't like the idea of a forgiving God. It seems as though God can't win!

Maybe this is because we think both can't exist simultaneously. We know we live in a broken world and long to see it made right. But we also know *we* are part of the problem. So the best we can do is point our finger at someone who's a "bigger problem" and tell God, "*That's who you really want to be angry with!*"

But there's a better way. When Jesus chose to go to the cross, he paid the price for the evil done to us *and* the evil we do to others. He set us free from judgment, and now we can use our freedom to love and sacrifice for others.

Without judgment, forgiveness is hollow and meaningless. Without forgiveness, judgment would doom us all. Judgment and forgiveness intersect at a place called grace.

 Questions to Ponder:

When are you least likely to want to pray? How can you be honest with God in those times?

Have you ever been uncomfortable with the idea of a judging God? Have you ever been uncomfortable with the idea of a forgiving God? Why are both needed for true grace to take place?

---

31 Jethani.

Day 32:
When God Bends His Knee

Today's Bible Reading: Jonah 4:4-11
Supporting Passage: Genesis 4:1-16

The LORD replied, "Is it right for you to be angry about this?"

I once saw a child throw a temper tantrum at Panera Bread. He and his mother were standing in line when he began jumping and screaming at the top of his lungs. Most parents would be mortified by this behavior and try their best to make a swift exit. But the mother remained calm. She bent down on one knee and began talking to her son gently.

"What's wrong?" she whispered.

I don't know what was said between mother and child, but the tantrum was soon calmed.

God reacts to our tantrums in the same tender way. He bends his knee and gets down on our level to calm us.

After Jonah finishes berating God for his compassion, God responds to Jonah with… *compassion*. He invites Jonah into a conversation by asking him a question: "Is it right for you to be angry about this?" (v. 4) God wants Jonah to dig deeper and explore where this anger inside of him is coming from.

Jonah refuses to give God an answer. Instead, he goes outside the city to be alone. It's almost like Jonah stomps into his room and slams the door in God's face! But God is a loving father who continues to pursue

Jonah. At the beginning of this story, God sent Jonah—the "dove"—as a peace offering to the Ninevites. Now God becomes a dove for Jonah. Will Jonah accept God's peace offering the way the Ninevites did?

This isn't the first time God tries to calm the anger of one of his beloved children. We see him do it throughout Scripture, going all the way back to the story of Cain and Abel. Most people are familiar with this tale of two brothers whose relationship gets poisoned by jealousy. When God accepts Abel's offering over Cain's, Cain becomes so enraged that he kills his brother. But before the murder happens, God responds to Cain's anger with compassion. He bends down on one knee to be at Cain's level. Then he whispers:

"Why are you so angry?" the LORD asked Cain. "Why do you look so dejected? You will be accepted if you do what is right. But if you refuse to do what is right, then watch out! Sin is crouching at the door, eager to control you. But you must subdue it and be its master." (Genesis 4:6-7, NLT)

In the middle of Cain's temper tantrum, God comes to him and says, "What have you got to be angry about? Look, the day isn't over yet. There's still time to make things right."

God extends a loving hand to Cain, but Cain swipes it away. He hatches a plan to lure his brother into a deserted field and kill him there. Unfortunately, Cain's pride causes him to reject God's offer of grace.

How will Jonah choose to respond to God's compassion? Over the coming days, we'll unpack the remaining verses of Jonah's story. We'll see God teach Jonah a poignant lesson through a cushy plant and a hungry worm. But today, I want to reflect on the tenderness God has for his children. It's a tenderness available to us when we feel the way Cain and Jonah did.

There are times I get so angry that I run into my proverbial room and slam the door in God's face. Then I hear God knocking. He comes in

DAY 32: WHEN GOD BENDS HIS KNEE

and gets down on one knee so he can look me in the eye. "It's okay, Michael," he whispers. "You think it's too late for a fresh start, but it's not. There's still time to turn things around."

The next time God bends his knee for me, I hope I set down my pride. I pray I have the humility to give God a bear hug, thank him for his amazing grace, and then joyfully run off to do what's right.

 Questions to Ponder:

What similarities do you see between Cain and Jonah? When are these traits most likely to come out in you?

Take some time to read Jonah 4:4-11 slowly. Where are the moments you see God "bending his knee" to get down to Jonah's level?

When has God bent his knee to talk to you in your anger? How did you respond?

Day 33:
A Shelter of Self-Righteousness

Today's Bible Reading: Jonah 4:5
Supporting Passage: Matthew 18:21-35

Then Jonah went out to the east side of the city and made a shelter to sit under as he waited to see what would happen to the city.

After God bends his knee and questions Jonah about his anger, Jonah refuses to respond. Instead, he goes outside the city and makes a shelter for himself. This shelter was probably a tiny hut made from interlaced tree branches.[32] It provided a bit of an escape from the brutal Assyrian sun. After building his hideout, Jonah settled in and waited to see what would happen to Nineveh.

But what was he waiting for? God had already decided to spare Nineveh. Was Jonah hoping the Ninevites would return to their evil ways so soon? (Or "repent again of their repentance," as poet John Carlisle put it.[33]) God didn't give up on the Ninevites. Apparently, Jonah wasn't about to either. He still had hope that they would mess things up and be destroyed! So Jonah kicked back and waited to see the drama unfold.

Like so many other times throughout this story, I see this pesky trait of Jonah's inside myself. How often do I enjoy watching drama unfold—drama that is none of my business? Sometimes I'll come across a heated Facebook thread and stop to gawk. I see people on both sides

---

32 Smith, p. 276.

33 Carlisle, Thomas John. *You! Jonah!* Eerdmans, 1968.

DAY 33: A SHELTER OF SELF-RIGHTEOUSNESS

of a debate making personal attacks. Things are getting ugly, so what do I do? *Grab the popcorn!* I may not add to the chaos, but I can't take my eyes off of it as I wait for the next juicy comment. It's so tempting to view the pain of others as a source of entertainment.

Jonah should have been inside the city, celebrating with the Ninevites and teaching them more about YHWH. Instead, he sat under a shelter of his own self-righteousness, seething at God's mercy. And the irony is, Jonah welcomed this mercy when he needed it two chapters ago. It seems we want mercy when *we* mess up, but justice when the mess belongs to others.

Jonah is like the main character in Jesus' parable of the unmerciful servant.[34] One day, the disciple Peter asks Jesus how many times he should forgive someone who wrongs him. Peter, thinking he was being generous, throws out the number seven as a good option. He was a bit off:

"No, not seven times," Jesus replied, "but seventy times seven!" (Matthew 18:22, NLT)

Jesus was telling Peter that forgiveness should be limitless. He then launches into a story about a servant who owes the king a crazy amount of money. His debt is impossible to pay off—it's equivalent to about twenty years' worth of wages. But the king takes mercy on the servant and frees him of his debt.

The servant skips off whistling a happy tune but then runs into another servant who happens to owe *him* money. The amount he's owed is significantly less than what he owed the king just moments before. But despite having received mercy himself, he opts to throw his buddy in jail until the debt can be paid. Jesus ends the tale this way:

"Then the king called in the man he had forgiven and said, 'You evil servant! I forgave you that tremendous debt because you pleaded with me. **Shouldn't you**

---

34 Keller, p. 114.

have mercy on your fellow servant, just as I had mercy on you?' *Then the angry king sent the man to prison to be tortured until he had paid his entire debt. That's what my heavenly Father will do to you if you refuse to forgive your brothers and sisters from your heart."* (Matthew 18:32-35, NLT, emphasis mine)

Jesus' story is simple, but it pierces our hearts. (He had a knack for doing that!) How can we accept God's mercy but then refuse to show mercy to others?

When Jonah was sinking into the sea, he cried out to God. God heard him and provided him the grace of a fish. To Jonah's credit, he was thankful. But now, when the Ninevites cry out to God, Jonah wants God to turn his back on them.

Once we construct a shelter of self-righteousness, it's hard to see people the way God sees them. So we need to bulldoze that shelter to the ground! And how do we do that?

By remembering how messy *we* are. By remembering how broken *we* are. And by remembering how much mercy God has given us, even though we didn't deserve it.

💬 Questions to Ponder:

When Jonah settled in to see what would happen to Nineveh, what do you think he was waiting for?

When are you most likely to "kick back and wait to watch the drama unfold"? In those moments, what would a more compassionate response be?

Have you constructed a shelter of self-righteousness in any area of your life? How is it affecting your view of others? Take some time today to remember the ways God has forgiven you.

Day 34:
Sometimes Grace Feels Like a Sunburn

Today's Bible Reading: Jonah 4:5-8

When the sun rose, God provided a scorching east wind, and the sun blazed on Jonah's head so that he grew faint. He wanted to die, and said, "It would be better for me to die than to live."

The word *grace* pops up a lot in Christian circles (including in this book's title!). It's an important word, but one that can lose its meaning if we don't stop to think about how incredible of a concept it is. A common definition of grace is that it's *the unmerited favor of God*. But what does that mean to you? What does God's grace feel like in your experience?

As we've seen from Jonah's story, God's grace may not always feel like grace at first. In chapter 2, Jonah learned that grace smells like fish guts. The fish that became Jonah's prison was also the fish God used to save Jonah from death. And now, in chapter 4, Jonah learns that grace sometimes feels like a sunburn.

After Jonah walks away from God, he builds a shelter to shield himself from the hot sun. But this hastily made hideout won't protect him for long. In Mesopotamia, average temperatures can get up to 110 F.[35] (As a fan of musicals, it makes me wonder if the show *110 in the Shade* should have been about Jonah!) As Jonah sat there stewing, beads of sweat started rolling down his face, agitating him even more.

Earlier, Jonah mocked God for being slow to anger with the Ninevites.

---
35   Smith, p. 278.

But now, Jonah becomes the benefactor of God's patience. Seeing Jonah in a grumpy mood, God "provided a leafy plant" (v. 6) to give him a bit of relief from the heat. The word "provided" is the same word used at the end of chapter 1 when God *provided* the fish for Jonah. It was an act of grace, and Jonah was "very happy" to accept God's compassion when it helped him.

Many commentators point out this is the first time Jonah is happy in the story. *Finally, something was going his way!* Jonah took comfort in the plant. And this, in itself, is not a bad thing. It's important to take care of ourselves. The problem comes when our comforts make us oblivious to the people around us.

Jonah enjoys the plant for the rest of the day and into the night. But the next morning, God "provided" Jonah with two more things that *didn't* make him so happy:

> *But at dawn the next day God **provided** a worm, which chewed the plant so that it withered. When the sun rose, God **provided** a scorching east wind, and the sun blazed on Jonah's head so that he grew faint. He wanted to die, and said, "It would be better for me to die than to live."* (Jonah 4:7-8, NIV, emphasis mine)

Why did God send a plant to ease Jonah's discomfort, only to then send a worm to destroy it? Was God paying Jonah back for his poor attitude? No. The worm and the blazing sun was an act of grace, just like the fish was. God was using them to reveal something *about* Jonah *to* Jonah.

While inside the fish, Jonah blasted the Ninevites for having idols (Day 19). But he couldn't see the idols he had constructed in his own life until God tore them down. We have the same problem. We typically think of "idols" as bad things. But an idol can be any good thing that we've made into an ultimate thing.

I like to start my mornings at Panera with an asiago bagel and a nice glass of sweet tea. (For those who don't live in the south, you may not understand how refreshing sweet tea can be. I pray God will *provide* you some.) It helps me get ready for the day. But if missing a morning at Panera makes me a miserable person to be around, then I've made it an idol in my life. (I wish that were a hypothetical situation, but sadly it's not.)

Grace doesn't always feel like grace. Sometimes God's grace reveals something in us we'd rather not see. But when that happens, it's not God's way of punishing us. It's his way of bringing it into the light so we can begin to deal with it.

Facing our idols can be scary. But when we face them with God, there's no guilt or shame. He knows we can't do it on our own. Only God's grace can change us.

 Questions to Ponder:

How would you define grace? Has grace felt different to you in different situations?

What do you think God was trying to teach Jonah through the plant and worm?

Is there anything in your life (even a good thing) that you've made into an ultimate thing? If so, how can you face it with God, knowing there's grace?

Day 35:
Never Too Late to Return Home (Part II)

Today's Bible Reading: Jonah 4:9
Supporting Passage: Luke 15:11-32

But God said to Jonah, "Is it right for you to be angry about the plant?"

When Jonah explodes in anger at the beginning of chapter 4, God asks him a question: "Is it right for you to be angry?" (v. 4, NIV)

At this point in his adventure, Jonah was facing severe exhaustion. First, he had been flung off a boat and swallowed by a fish. Then he traveled hundreds of miles to deliver an emotionally draining message in Nineveh. And now, the relentless heat was starting to get to him. Maybe Jonah didn't have the mental energy to face God's question.

That's when God tries a different tactic. He grows a plant over Jonah and uses it as an object lesson. After giving Jonah time to cool off (both literally and figuratively), God takes the plant away from him. Then he asks Jonah the same question, but with a twist: "Is it right for you to be angry *about the plant?*" (v. 9, NIV, emphasis mine)

God was saying to Jonah, "Okay, let's forget about Nineveh for a moment. Instead, let's focus on this plant you suddenly love so much. Is it right for you to be angry about *that?*"

This time Jonah breaks his silence and answers God's question:

"It is," he said. "And I'm so angry I wish I were dead." (v. 9, NIV)

DAY 35: NEVER TOO LATE TO RETURN HOME (PART II)

Jonah is still angry. But is the plant really what he's angry about? Or is there something more going on inside of Jonah?

Could it be that maybe Jonah was feeling some anger toward *himself*? Maybe Jonah looked back on his adventure and felt like he blew it big time. He got a second chance after running from God only to mess up again in Nineveh. The journey had revealed some ugliness in him, and he didn't think there was a way back home.

On Day 18 we looked at the younger brother in the parable of the prodigal son. He ran away from his father because he wanted to live life his own way. But when he woke up in a pigsty, he was jolted back to reality. Sometimes we run from God the "younger brother" way. When we get a mouthful of pig slop, it's easy to recognize how lost we are.

But there is also a more subtle way of running. It's the kind of running we do without ever leaving home. It's the "older brother" way of running from God.

When the father throws a welcome home party for his younger son, the older son refuses to attend. So the father leaves the party and pleads with him. He reminds his firstborn, "You are always with me, and everything I have is yours" (Luke 15:31, NIV).

Over the years, the older brother became lost without ever leaving home. The joy of working for his father became an obligation. He may have been physically present, but in his mind he was a million miles away. Now his father was extending an invitation to return home. The father wants to throw him a celebration too.

As the older brother listened to his father's pleas, I wonder if something in him wanted to join the party. Maybe at this moment, the older brother wished he could embrace his father the way the younger brother did. But he stood there frozen because of his shame and embarrassment.

The younger brother traveled hundreds of miles back to his father. The older brother was only three steps away, but his feet felt as heavy as lead.

I've been there. Sometimes I know I'm acting as ridiculous as Jonah and the older brother. I say I'm angry about the situation, but secretly, I'm mad *at myself* for the way I've acted. My insides are churning with equal parts shame, pride, and self-loathing. I feel like a disappointment. So I dig in my heels because I think it's too late to make peace with God and others.

If it were too late, the father would have shut the doors to the party and left the older brother outside. But he didn't.

If it were too late, God would have left Jonah to sulk by himself outside the city gates of Nineveh. But he didn't.

The journey back home may look different for older and younger brothers because their messes are different.

But God doesn't want either one left out.

 Questions to Ponder:

What's the difference between the "younger brother" way of running and the "older brother" way of running? Which one do you relate to more?

Where do you think Jonah's anger was coming from?

Have you ever let anger or embarrassment at your own behavior prevent you from reconciling with God and others? In those moments, how can you take one step toward home even though your feet may feel like lead?

Day 36:
The Wrong Way To Do Religion

Today's Bible Reading: Jonah 4:10-11
Supporting Passage: John 13

"And should I not have concern for the great city of Nineveh …?"

It's hard to believe our adventure with Jonah is almost at its end. The book of Jonah concludes with God getting the last words. *And oh, what words they are!* These final words are amazing. They are also a bit unsettling for anyone who follows God.

After Jonah tells God that yes, it *is* right for him to be angry at the withered plant, God speaks these words:

But the LORD said, "You have been concerned about this plant, though you did not tend it or make it grow. It sprang up overnight and died overnight. And should I not have concern for the great city of Nineveh, in which there are more than a hundred and twenty thousand people who cannot tell their right hand from their left—and also many animals?" (Jonah 4:10-11, NIV)

Jonah has been living under the assumption that God's love is reserved for the people who look like Jonah and think like Jonah. So he took the liberty of drawing the boundary lines *for* God. He knew who was in and who was out. But this whole adventure has forced Jonah to rethink all that. God's love is bigger than any label we place on others (or they place on themselves).

Through these tender words, God communicates his deep love for the Ninevites. When he says there are people in Nineveh "who cannot tell their right hand from their left," you get a sense he feels sorry for them. (And in the NLT, God's final words are translated, "Shouldn't I feel sorry for such a great city?") God is not excusing their violence. And he's not saying they are oblivious, either. If the Ninevites gave up their evil ways, then they *knew* their ways were evil.

But on another level, the Ninevites were misguided and didn't know the way back home. This is the tension we feel when we look at the world. Wherever there is violence, there is lostness. So God grieved for Nineveh's victims, but he also grieved for Nineveh.

And then, in a book full of ironic moments, the author throws in one final punch. God ends his speech by talking about his love for Nineveh's animals. I think this was a little inside joke between God and Jonah. God smiled and said, "Hey Jonah… Remember when the Ninevites made their animals fast? And you laughed to yourself, thinking how stupid that was, but you didn't step in to teach them anything? *Well, guess what?* I even care about those poor, hungry animals!"

These final words from God uncomfortably redefine what "religion" is. It's not just about our relationship with God. It's about our relationship with others and how we love them. The two are intertwined.

Centuries after Jonah, when God put on skin and came to live with us, he doubled down on this idea. This time it was hundreds of miles away from Nineveh, in a small upper room in Jerusalem. Jesus and the disciples were celebrating the Passover meal together. Then, out of nowhere, Jesus got up and started washing his friends' stinky feet. The same feet that would run away from him a few hours later when things got real. Jesus was about to sacrifice everything to show his love to the world—a world full of people different from us. And he spoke these words:

"A new command I give you: Love one another. As I have loved you, so you must love one another. By this everyone will know that you are my disciples, if you love one another." (John 13:34-35, NIV)

DAY 36: THE WRONG WAY TO DO RELIGION

These words, like the ones God spoke to Jonah, leave me feeling unsettled. I would rather say a few prayers, tick off a few boxes, and know I'm right with God. But God wants me to stop looking up and start looking into the eyes of the people across from me.

This morning, I woke up to see an unkind comment on one of my Facebook posts. It's amazing how deep nine small words can cut. I shot off a snarky response without thinking and regretted it later. I wish I would have taken the time to see that person the way God sees them.

It will always feel cleaner to keep things between God and me. Loving others—especially those we see as "outsiders"—gets messy because people are messy. But if our version of religion prevents us from loving others, then we are doing it the wrong way.[36]

 Questions to Ponder:

How do you interpret God's final words to Jonah? Do you see a connection between those words and Jesus' words in John 13?

What do you think God meant when he said there were Ninevites who "cannot tell their right hand from their left"? What do you think it looks like to hold people accountable for their actions yet also grieve for them?

Who do you label as "outsiders"? Have you ever used your commitment to God as an excuse not to show compassion to them?

---

36 This is a paraphrase of a statement made by Pastor Andy Stanley, and I want to give him proper credit! The main idea of today's devotional was heavily influenced by him.

Day 37:
When God Loves My Enemy, It's Good News for Me

Today's Bible Reading: Jonah 4:10-11
Supporting Passages: Luke 2:8-20

But the LORD said, "You have been concerned about this plant, though you did not tend it or make it grow... And should I not have concern for the great city of Nineveh...?"

Yesterday we looked at how God grieved for the city of Nineveh. He didn't excuse or overlook their violent ways, yet his heart broke for their lostness. By contrast, Jonah's heart grew cold toward the Ninevites.

The word translated as "concerned" in the last two verses of Jonah can be expressed as "have compassion."[37] It's an emotional response. God is telling Jonah, "Look, you have compassion for this plant even though you have no real connection to it. That's fine. But if that's true, shouldn't I have compassion for a whole city of people? People I created and love?"

Jonah had more affection for a plant than for people. But it wasn't *totally* about the plant, was it? Yes, Jonah was happy the plant provided him with shade. But Jonah's true affection—the thing he valued above everything else—was his perspective of how the world worked. (Or how the world *should* work if it were up to him.) Jonah had it all figured out.

---

37 Smith, p. 281.

DAY 37: WHEN GOD LOVES MY ENEMY, IT'S GOOD NEWS FOR ME

This is an easy trap to fall into, especially when there are divided opinions on everything. We get emotional about causes, ideas, politics, and viewpoints. This is not a bad thing in itself. God wants us to care about the issues going on in the world. But if we allow these things to capture the top spot in our hearts, we lose compassion for people. We begin to see those we disagree with as enemies to defeat instead of people to love. And, like Jonah, we put limits on who deserves God's grace.

But nobody *deserves* God's grace! That's why the gospel is good news for all people. And on the night Jesus was born, God sent angels to tell this news to some lowly shepherds:

"Don't be afraid!" [the angel] said. "I bring you good news that will bring great joy to all people. The Savior—yes, the Messiah, the Lord—has been born today in Bethlehem, the city of David! And you will recognize him by this sign: You will find a baby wrapped snugly in strips of cloth, lying in a manger." (Luke 2:10-12, NLT)

Many scholars say shepherds were outcasts in ancient Jerusalem. Others call that view exaggerated. Either way, shepherds were ordinary people doing their best to get by in life. And God chose them to be the first people to hear about this newborn Savior. If Jesus came for stinky, messy shepherds, then that was good news for royalty as well. But it was only good news if they recognized that—underneath the gold garments—*they* were stinky and messy too.

Jonah thought God's love for Nineveh was a slap in the face to his own people. After all, what had the Ninevites ever done for God? But God was trying to show Jonah that his love for Nineveh was good news for *everyone*.

When the father throws a party for the younger brother, it's good news for the older brother. It means he can feel secure in his father's love, too.

As Jonah sat there under his broken shelter, God wrapped an arm around him and whispered, "Come on, Jonah. Let's go down there and celebrate with the Ninevites. I love them just like I love you. My love is big enough for everyone. And you need my grace as much as they do."

When God loves my enemy, it's good news for me.

But it's only good news if I recognize that—underneath all my self-righteousness—*I'm* as stinky and messy as they are.

 Questions to Ponder:

Why was God's compassion for Nineveh good news for Jonah? Why is God's compassion for your enemies (or people you disagree with) good news for you?

Has any idea or viewpoint captured the ultimate affection of your heart? If so, how does it affect the way you interact with other people? Take some time today to ask Jesus to help you reorder those affections.

Take a moment to reread Jonah 4. What is one thing you've learned from this section of the story?

Day 38:
Step Into Jonah's Shoes

Today's Bible Reading: Jonah 1-4
Supporting Passage: Luke 15

We've made it through our adventure with Jonah! If you've stuck with me this far, I want to say thank you. I had so much fun journeying through the book of Jonah, and I hope you did too. We'll spend our final three days zooming out to take a big picture look at this story.

As we saw yesterday, the book of Jonah is good news for all people. But it's only good if I see myself as messy and broken. I need God's grace as much as anyone else does. As the book ends, God desperately tries to get Jonah to understand this. Looking out over Nineveh, God whispers to Jonah:

"You have been concerned about this plant, though you did not tend it or make it grow. It sprang up overnight and died overnight. And should I not have concern for the great city of Nineveh, in which there are more than a hundred and twenty thousand people who cannot tell their right hand from their left—and also many animals?" (Jonah 4:10–11, NIV)

With these words, God invites Jonah to lay down his self-righteousness and celebrate with the Ninevites. All eyes are on Jonah now as we wait to hear his response. What's his next move?

We don't know!

The book abruptly ends with God's question. We flip to the next page, searching for Jonah's answer, but it's nowhere to be found. For a book filled with so much excitement, it's a pretty anticlimactic ending. (If Jonah were a TV series, I'm sure it'd be up there with *Lost*, *Seinfield*, and *The Sopranos* for most disappointing finales.) But the author of Jonah knew what he was doing.

Back on Day 3, I said the book of Jonah is all about *us*. We've seen Jonah make a lot of mistakes over the past few weeks. But with each mistake comes the opportunity to step into Jonah's shoes and see how we fall into the same traps. It's also a reminder that no matter how bad we mess up, God offers us waves and waves of grace. God's grace chases after us when we run away. It follows us down into the depths of the murky sea. And it tenderly wraps an arm around our shoulder when we let anger consume us.

And now, before we close the book, the author offers us one final chance to step into Jonah's shoes. Tim Mackie says the book of Jonah holds a mirror up to the reader. It forces us to grapple with the question, "Am I okay with God showing love to my enemies?"[38]

Jesus may have drawn inspiration from Jonah when he told his prodigal son story. It ends the same way, with the father inviting the older son to lay down his self-righteousness.

> *"My son,"* the father said, *"you are always with me, and everything I have is yours. But we had to celebrate and be glad, because this brother of yours was dead and is alive again; he was lost and is found."* (Luke 15:31–31, NIV)

As with Jonah, we never hear how the older brother responds. Did he join the party and make peace with his little brother? Or did he stay outside, seething with anger? Jesus invited his audience to step into the older brother's shoes and decide for themselves. And this invitation is even more profound when we consider *who* was listening to Jesus' story.

In Luke 15, Jesus tells a series of three parables about missing things

---

38 BibleProject. "Overview: Jonah."

DAY 38: STEP INTO JONAH'S SHOES

that get found and celebrated. He starts with the parable of the lost sheep and then moves on to the lost coin. His grand finale is the most well-known of the three, the prodigal son. But why did Jesus launch into this grace-filled storytime? Luke tells us the reason at the start of the chapter:

Tax collectors and other notorious sinners often came to listen to Jesus teach. This made the Pharisees and teachers of religious law complain that he was associating with such sinful people—even eating with them! So Jesus told them this story... (Luke 15:1–3, NLT)

Jesus was spending time with sinners and it drove the Pharisees crazy. And so, Jesus tells a trifecta of stories to remind them of the beauty of God's grace. While anyone in the room could benefit from hearing these stories (notorious sinners included!), Jesus was trying to penetrate the hearts of the religious leaders. These men became so preoccupied with religion that they were missing the joy happening right in front of them.

I think anyone—no matter what they believe about God—can learn something from the book of Jonah. But the final verses are not written to atheists or unbelievers. They are addressed to the "good" people who follow YHWH. God's words challenge those of us who've gotten too comfortable with religion.

As I step into Jonah's shoes, the question becomes aimed at me.

Will I lay down my self-righteousness and love my enemy the way God loves them?

> 💬 **Questions to Ponder:**
>
> Read through the book of Jonah one more time. (I know, by now you might be sick of it!) In each scene, put yourself in Jonah's shoes. What have you learned about yourself through Jonah's adventure?
>
> Is there any area of your life where you need to lay down your self-righteousness? What steps can you take to do that?

Day 39:
Maybe a Happy Ending After All?

The word of the LORD came to Jonah son of Amittai...

Yesterday we considered what the end of the book of Jonah means for us. The ending is left unresolved because we now stand in Jonah's shoes. What matters is not what Jonah did next but what *we* do next. Even so, we can't help but wonder what became of him. So today, I'm going to give my theory on why there may be a happy ending for ol' Jonah after all!

At the beginning of our adventure, we discussed what kind of literature the book of Jonah is. Most scholars say it falls into one of two general categories: It's either historical narrative or historical parable. (For a refresher on those two genres, skim through Day 2 again.) I believe the Jonah story is historical, but I also think it was written in a way that punches up the irony and humor. And here's the shocking reason why I have this view:

I think the author of the book of Jonah is... *Jonah himself!*

Is your mind blown?! *(Forgive me if I'm being overly dramatic with this reveal.)*

Full disclosure: I may be in the minority with this view. Most scholars doubt Jonah wrote the book himself. But some affirm he at least shared his story, and it was later written down by someone else.[39] One commentator argues Jonah would have never written a book "so consistently critical" of himself.[40] I think the opposite is true. The people

---
39 H.L. Ellison, "Jonah," EBC (Grand Rapids: Zondervan, 1985), 7:362.
40 Stuart, 432

who wrote the Bible did not hide their brokenness to make themselves look better. Jonah painted himself as a bumbling buffoon because he finally understood God's grace. He wasn't afraid to tell the world how big of a mess he was. When you've been to the depths of the ocean and back, there's nothing left to hide!

One person who *does* share the "Jonah as author" view is Timothy Keller. His book *The Prodigal Prophet* has been an incredible resource to me as I wrote this devotional. At the end of the book, Keller gives his opinion of what happened to Jonah. The following quote is lengthy, but it sums up why there might be a happy ending after all:

I propose ... that we can make a reasonable guess about how Jonah responded to God. How do we know Jonah was so recalcitrant, defiant, and clueless? How do we know that he made the unbelievable "I hate the God of love" speech? How do we know about his prayer inside the fish? The only way we could possibly know these things is if Jonah told others. What kind of man would let the world see what a fool he was? Only someone who had become joyfully secure in God's love. Only someone who believed that he was simultaneously sinful but completely accepted. In short, someone who has found in the gospel of grace the very power of God (Romans 1:16). If it can change Jonah, it can change anyone. It can change you.[41]

Of course, there's no way of knowing how Jonah's story ended. But if I were to write a bit of fan fiction, here's how it would go:

"Should I not have concern for the great city of Nineveh?" God asks Jonah.

Jonah sits with God's question for a while, thinking back on his adventure and the waves of grace shown to him. Then he gets up, brushes the dirt off his lap, and walks back into the city of Nineveh. He embraces his enemies with a hug. He laughs with the Ninevites. He cries with them. He throws a party and celebrates that what was lost has now been found. And part of what has been found is Jonah himself.

---

41 Keller, pp. 227-228

DAY 39: MAYBE A HAPPY ENDING AFTER ALL?

Then Jonah returns home and tells his story to everyone he meets. His friends are shocked.

"Is this really Jonah?" they whisper to each other. "The same guy who gleefully predicted Assyria's doom?"

"If you tell this story to anyone else, make sure you leave out the 'running away from God' part," they warn him. "It doesn't make you look good at all. Hurts credibility."

"I'd be embarrassed if I were you!" they chide.

But for some reason, Jonah can't help but smile as he tells every embarrassing detail. He seems to relish in making himself the butt of every joke.

Jonah is not the same person he was when he began this adventure. His greatest fear has come true. But it's also become the thing that has set him free: Jonah finally realizes he's a messy, broken person. Just like the Ninevites. Just like you and me.

Jonah lets out a sigh of relief. He can rest in God's love. And that makes him want to share it with everyone he meets.

Yes, he's learned God doesn't want anyone left out!

 Questions to Ponder:

What do you think happened to Jonah after his adventure in Nineveh?

Can you think of other Bible stories that don't try to clean up the faults of their "heroes"?

How has God's grace changed you?

Day 40:
The Good Epilogue

Today's Bible Reading: Luke 10:25-37

"Then a despised Samaritan came along, and when he saw the man, he felt compassion for him..."

Yesterday, we considered the possibility of a happy ending for Jonah. His adventure in Nineveh showed the power of God's grace in both Jonah's life and the Ninevites'. But as transforming as it was, it didn't heal the animosity between Israel and Assyria. Time goes on, and if we're not actively working on loving and serving others, it's easy to slip into old ways of living.

Several decades after Jonah, Assyria conquered the northern kingdom of Israel. Many Israelites were taken back to Assyria as prisoners. But some of the Assyrians stayed in Israel and intermarried with the Jews. This was an act of aggression on Assyria's part—a way to strip the Jewish people of their national identity. The offspring of the Jews and Assyrians became known as Samaritans.[42] (Samaria was the capital city of the northern kingdom.)

Why is this significant? Because it means Samaritans were partial descendants of the Ninevites! The hatred between Israel and Nineveh continued but became more complicated. These two nations were now forever connected.

---

42   Roat, Alyssa. "The Samaritans: Hope from the History of a Hated People." *Biblestudytools.com*, Salem Web Network, 10 Feb. 2020, https://www.biblestudytools.com/bible-study/topical-studies/the-samaritans-hope-from-the-history-of-a-hated-people.html.

DAY 40: THE GOOD EPILOGUE

Fast forward to hundreds of years later. The Jews and Samaritans were still at odds with each other. By this time, the Samaritans formed a new religion that was kind of like Judaism but also kind of... *not*. They had their own temple and way of worshiping God. The Jews considered the Samaritans half-breeds—worse than pagans. So they did whatever they could to stay separated from them. (And before we feel tempted to judge, let's keep in mind all the groups of people *we* try to avoid!)

Then a guy named Jesus comes to town. And under the backdrop of all this bad blood, he tells the story of the good Samaritan. (But Jesus didn't call it that because if he did, people would have tuned him out before he started.)

Most people know the basic premise of the good Samaritan even if they've never read the Bible. A man gets beaten up by robbers and left for dead along a roadside. Two people pass him by without helping. But then a third person comes along and nurses him back to health. It's a nice story about helping others even when we're busy. But there's a deeper layer of meaning underneath the surface.

The man who got attacked was Jewish. The two people who passed him by without a second glance were his own countrymen. The only person who would offer help was "a *despised* Samaritan" (v. 31, NLT).

This was shocking and offensive to the people listening to Jesus. After studying Jonah's story, we can begin to understand why. This would be like Jonah getting beat up on his way to Nineveh and being rescued by a despised Ninevite!

As with the prodigal son, Jesus had his audience in mind when he told this tale. It began with a question thrown at Jesus by a man who was good at being good:

One day an expert in religious law stood up to test Jesus by asking him this question: "Teacher, what should I do to inherit eternal life?"

Jesus replied, "What does the law of Moses say? How do you read it?"

The man answered, "'You must love the Lord your God with all your heart, all your soul, all your strength, and all your mind.' And, 'Love your neighbor as yourself.'"

"Right!" Jesus told him. "Do this and you will live!"

The man wanted to justify his actions, so he asked Jesus, "And who is my neighbor?" (Luke 10:25–29, NLT)

This religious expert—like Jonah centuries before him—thought there was an "in" group and an "out" group. He's okay with loving people as long as they are on a pre-approved list of lovable people. "Who is my neighbor?" was code for, "Hey Jesus, who am I allowed to *not* love?"

But Jesus rips that list to shreds. He redefines our neighbor to be anyone and everyone. It's the people who are different from us. It's the people we pass by without helping because they probably made their mess themselves. It's the people we deem as being "what's wrong with our world/country/city today."

After Jesus ends his story, he throws the question back on the man:

"Now which of these three would you say was a neighbor to the man who was attacked by bandits?" Jesus asked.

The man replied, "The one who showed him mercy."

Then Jesus said, "Yes, now go and do the same." (Luke 10:36–37, NLT)

We are messy, broken people who have received waves of grace from God.

Now we are called to go love others the way he loves us.

So let's make some waves!

DAY 40: THE GOOD EPILOGUE

💬 Questions to Ponder:

What similarities do you see between Jonah's story and the parable of the good Samaritan? Does knowing the backstory of Samaritans change the way you understand it?

Looking back on our adventure with Jonah, what is your biggest takeaway? Is there a next step God is asking you to take?

The Next (Messy) Adventure Awaits...

Thank you for going on this adventure with me (and Jonah!) over the past 40 days. I hope it's helped you gain a new perspective on a familiar tale. The book of Jonah isn't about a fish swallowing a man. It's about a man discovering the depths of God's love for messy, broken people. And you know what? Jonah isn't the only messy person in the Bible. Far from it!

The Bible is full of stories about God loving and including messy, broken people. Every week or so, I write an article about one of these stories. If you'd like to receive them in your inbox, I invite you to sign up for my free Nobody Left Out newsletter. Subscribers will also be the first to know about new book releases and other content I produce. You can subscribe at NobodyLeftOut.net.

As our adventure with Jonah ends, I hope we'll embark on a new one. I hope we'll be bold enough to cross lines and love people who are different from us. We ended our 40-day journey by looking at Jesus' parable of the good Samaritan. For Jesus, the story was more than just a nice idea. He lived it out and tore down barriers wherever he went.

In John 4, Jesus strikes up a conversation with a woman he meets at a well. This was scandalous on multiple levels. Not only was it culturally taboo for a man to speak to a woman in public, but this woman was... a despised *Samaritan*! The woman knew how bad this looked for both of them:

The woman was surprised, for Jews refuse to have anything to do with Samaritans.

She said to Jesus, "You are a Jew, and I am a Samaritan woman. Why are you asking me for a drink?" (John 4:9, NLT)

The disciples are also stunned when they find Jesus having this interaction. But after their conversation, the woman runs back to her town and tells everyone about Jesus. And something incredible happens:

Many Samaritans from the village believed in Jesus because the woman had said, "He told me everything I ever did!" When they came out to see him, they begged him to stay in their village. So he stayed for two days, long enough for many more to hear his message and believe. (John 4:39–41, NLT)

The disciples must have been mortified to see so many Samaritans running to Jesus. But I'm sure Jesus had a big smile on his face, just as God did when the Ninevites ran to him.

Of course, you know what I'm going to say, right?

I've said it so many times in this book, but I can't think of a better way to end it.

God really doesn't want anyone left out!

The Nobody Left Out Series

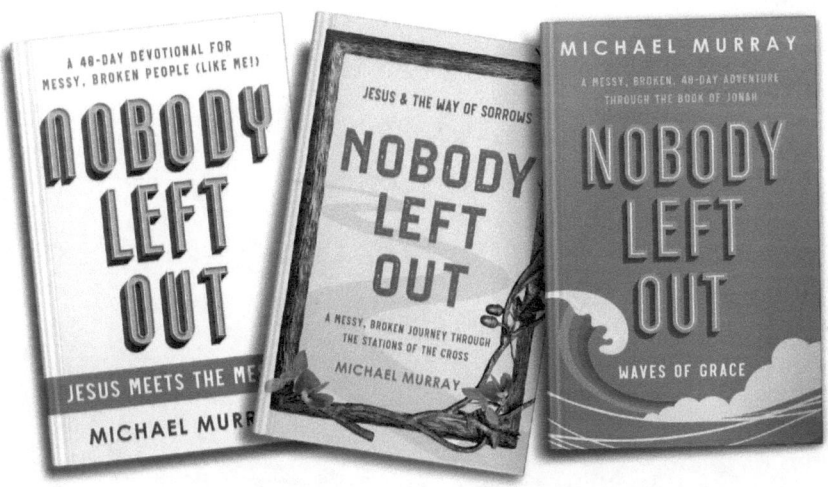

Check out the entire *Nobody Left Out* devotional series at:

NobodyLeftOut.Net/Series

A Small Favor...

Thank you so much for reading *Nobody Left Out: Waves of Grace*. Now that you've finished reading it, I would love to get your thoughts. It would mean a lot to me if you left an honest review wherever you picked this book up.

As you may know, reviews play an essential role in reaching other readers. They help people decide whether or not this book is right for them. Reviews also help me gain insight into the things I got right, and the areas I need to improve. I want to get better as a writer!

Based on your review, I'll continue tweaking this book's content and putting out new editions. It will also help me as I write future devotional books.

Thank you!

About The Author

Michael Murray is just a messy, broken guy trying to follow Jesus one step at a time. He was born with cerebral palsy, a disability that affects motor skills. Living life with CP has given Michael a unique perspective on God's grace and mercy. He created the *Nobody Left Out* book series to share the good news that every single person matters to Jesus.

Michael and his wife Diana live in Orlando, Florida, with their son Emmett and dog Ruby. (Diana is an amazing artist!) He attends Summit Church and is a big fan of sweet tea, musicals, and writing about himself in the third person.

Connect with Michael:

Website: **NobodyLeftOut.net**
YouTube Channel: YouTube.com/MichaelMurrayIsMessy
Facebook: Facebook.com/NobodyLeftOut
Instagram: Instagram.com/MichaelJMurray83

Special Thanks

I hesitate to write a "thank you" section because I'm always afraid I will leave someone out (which would reflect poorly on my "Nobody Left Out" theme!). Even so, there are a few people I need to thank because without them, this book wouldn't have been possible.

Thank you to Dave Dickens and John K. Adams for looking over this book while it was in the "pre-editing" stage. The insights you provided were invaluable, and I appreciate the time and effort you took to comb through it.

Emily Lupfer, thank you for being a fantastic editor! (Fun fact: Emily was one of my co-writers for the *Jonah & the Wave Breakers* musical I referenced on Day 21.) I hope you had fun revisiting this crazy story. Thank you for catching all my mistakes and correcting my verb tenses when I can't decide if I'm writing in the past or present. I hope you decide to continue editing my books when you're on Broadway!

I need to give a huge thanks to Rob, Kristie, Vanessa, Tyler, and the entire team at Archangel Ink. They designed this book's cover and interior layout and are true gems to work with. They always respond with kindness and patience to every neurotic request I make of them. (Like, *Can you move that subtitle 1/1000th of an inch to the left???*) They offer an amazing service to self-publishers.

And speaking of self-publishing, I need to thank my mentor Dale L. Roberts. Dale, you've taught me so much about self-publishing over the past couple of years. I don't know where I'd be without your guidance and support. To anyone who dreams of publishing a book, be sure to check out the Self-Publishing with Dale YouTube channel.

The entire indie author community is full of awesome people. I want to give a shout-out to the friends I've made along the way, especially Andy Wen, Nick Nawroth (AKA "Papa Paws"), and Lori Rea. You are all incredible authors, and I am humbled by your friendship.

Bob Eichelberger, thank you for meeting me at Panera for breakfast every Tuesday morning and encouraging me in this journey. Your friendship means more to me than you know.

Mom, Dad, Darling, and Faith, thank you for always supporting me in everything I do. God has blessed me with an amazing family, and I love each one of you.

To all my blog readers, thank you for allowing me to "test" this material on you. All my books start out as blog posts, and I love receiving your comments and feedback. It helps me immensely as I begin turning it into a book. I appreciate all your encouragement and support.

Ahhh! So many more people to thank. *This* is why I didn't want to get started! But I'll end by thanking my wife, Diana, and son, Emmett. Thank you for putting up with me as I frantically pace around the house, trying to find the right words to put in this book. I love you guys!

And, of course...

God, thank you for loving me in my mess and being patient with me. I'm grateful you've invited me to be part of your story.